Mystical Empress Magical Relationships

Quantum Techniques to Enhance Relationships

Mystical Empress Brenda Renee'

Mystical Empress Publishing, LLC
Arvada, Colorado

Published and distributed in the United States by: Mystical Empress Publishing, LLC,

6002 Field Street, Arvada, CO 80004, (720)965-0062,

www.mysticalempresspublishing.com

Library of Congress Cataloguing-in-Publications Data

Renee', Brenda

Mystical Empress Magical Relationships/Brenda Renee.

p. cm.

Includes bibliographical references

ISBN 978-0-692-98602-8

1. Relationships 2. Quantum Physics

3. Astrology 4. Psychic Perceptions

Library of Congress Control Number: 2017918213

ISBN 978-0-692-98602-8

Printed in the United States of America

☆ *Deep Mystical Appreciation to* ☆

God, Creator of All Things, for the gifts of quantum physics and psychic perceptions.

Buckie, the tenacious crab for his unending patience, support, guidance, and strength

My trusting and loyal clients who helped weave these magical threads

My wise, enlightened teachers, who taught me in books, in person, and beyond the veil:

My Inner Counself ☆
Linda Goodman
The Animal, Plant, & Mineral Kingdom, Fairy Folk, Angels and Star-beings
Seth/Jane Roberts & Rob Butts
Sonia Choquette
Jean Avery ☆
Donna Cunningham
John Lonehawk Minerich
Silver Haired Wolf
Terah Kathryn Collins
Terry Lamb
Ted Andrews
Abraham-Hicks ☆
Eckhart Tolle
"What the Bleep Do We Know? Down the Rabbit Hole Quantum Edition"™

And….
Neville Goddard…thank you for your blessing beyond the veil ☆

This book is lovingly dedicated to

☆   Matt   ☆

You are the love of my life, my Buckie, my Puff-a-Lump, my lover, my husband, my best friend, my business partner, and my soul's eternal mate. You are my everything!

Thank you so much for loving me and sharing your life with me.

"I have loved you for a thousand years, and I'll love you for a thousand more."

Je t'adore! SCHNARFF!!!

"All the world's a stage
And all the men and women merely players;
They have their exits and their entrances;
And one man in his time plays many parts,
His acts being seven ages."

"As You Like It," Shakespeare

Table of Contents

A note from the Mystical Empress

In writing this book, I wanted to give you an entirely new magical model for all relationships. This book is not defined by age, gender, or sexual orientation. In your human experience, you engage many kinds of relationships.

For those who are searching for love, I offer you a definable road map with many hidden treasures. For those who desire positive changes in their current, personal and professional relationships, I offer you tools for harmony & longevity. For those who have loved & lost, I offer you renewed hope for finding what was thought to be lost.

As I never quite saw myself a teacher of relationships, I merely followed my passionate desire for my own joyful, connected relationship. I spent years sampling a variety of experiences, constantly refining myself & my desires, until I came upon my life partner, and soul mate, Matt, who had agreed in our soul contract to offer me the gift of understanding energy in relationships. He allowed me to move within new identities & new realities, to arrive at my wonderful dream of relationship. The techniques I created are what this book is about—my personal discoveries in molding energy as it pertains to relationships.

Before we get started, I do want to confirm that, yes, creating your ideal relationships will be work. Judging by the volume of relationship calls that I receive, I'd say this is the top focus in most peoples' minds. So, if you're going to relate, you may as well understand how to create happy, fulfilling relationships, right? Right!

My wish for you? The courage and focus to create and achieve all your relationship dreams.

They must often change, who would be constant in happiness or wisdom.
Confucius

Many Magical & Mystical Blessings,

Brenda Renee', Mystical Empress

My Introduction to Quantum Physics

Once upon a midnight dreary, while I pondered,
weak and weary...
suddenly there came a tapping, as of someone
gently rapping...

"The Raven", Edgar Allen Poe

Relationship as a Laboratory

My spiritual path began by reading *Linda Goodman's Star Signs*. I remember reading Linda's book in my early 20's and fearing that I was going against my Christian beliefs. Linda wrote in such way that she inspired me with a desire to learn more. Then, during my Saturn return**, I started reading Jane Robert's channeled, non-physical entity named Seth. Linda's writing was beautifully poetic, dotted with many riddles & mysteries, while Seth was very scientific and methodical. Seth was very deep and sometimes difficult to comprehend. Somehow, though, I knew his books were magic! As I flipped through the pages, I knew I was learning the secrets of the universe. My passionate drive to learn more pushed me to break from convention and study metaphysical and spiritual studies.

From the earliest age, I was always viewed as a leader and a guide by my peers. My years spent in study, introspection, and meditation, eventually evolved into a career as an intuitive, life

---

** Saturn return is an astrological cycle that occurs roughly every 28-30 years of life. At this time, Saturn returns to the position it occupied at the individual's birth. During the first and most important return, the individual goes through a crisis of consciousness. They prepare for adulthood by making major life decisions. It sets the tone for much of the adult path.

coach, shaman, and astrologer. My studies helped me to teach and guide others who needed answers.

When asked by clients, "How do you learn what you know? How do you grow psychically and spiritually?" I respond with a warning: "Be careful of what you seek. As you progress down the path of wisdom, you will eventually come to a fork in the road that will require a decision. You will choose to turn away from blossoming wisdom, in favor of old belief systems (i.e., someone else's truth), OR you will courageously push through fear to discover your own truth. For once you know something, you cannot unknow it. The "knowing" makes it very difficult to return to the old life dynamics."

My crossroads came when I went to my first class-reunion, during my Saturn return. I found myself in what I thought to be a delightful philosophical conversation with a man; however, I became a wee bit tipsy and said a little too much in the way of shamanic soul retrievals. The next day, at the class picnic, I learned that man was a Baptist deacon and had told all my friends that I was a witch who did rituals. This may not sound like much to you, but this was the Bible belt South. I left the picnic in humiliation and tears. That night as I went to sleep, I prayed: "God, if what I'm learning is wrong, I will burn all of my books and never look back. If I'm on track, I will move forward. Please give me a dream to let me know." The next morning, I recalled my dream: I was in a town of people who were like zombies. They all thought and acted alike and wanted me to conform. I ran through the town looking for someone to help me. I came upon a judge who tried to subdue me long enough for the mob to catch me. From that dream forward, I never looked back on my decision to pursue my quest for spiritual knowledge. Instead, I moved forward with great passion and fervor! Looking back, if I had not made that decision, a major part of me would've died. I was born to do the work that I do today.

Years later, I unknowingly stepped into the quantum lunatic fringe in the field of acting. I very naturally took to theater and film where I could apply my psychological insights to my characters & their lives. During an audition for a play, I met my first soul mate. I will never forget the moment I laid eyes on him. A handsome guy; he strolled in the theater, complaining about his father, and his arrogant, cocky demeanor won my immediate contempt. "Josh" reminded me of one of those "buff," self-absorbed villains who vies for the attention of the lead character's love interest. On stage, I wanted nothing to do with him, and he constantly picked on me. There was something about him though, that I could not shake. He filled my thoughts almost constantly. Once the play had run its course, I thought I was finished with him. Goodbye & good riddance!

Three months later, a local filmmaker was holding auditions for an independent film. When I arrived for the audition, Josh was sitting at a table, smug as usual. I considered walking away from the part, but I decided I would not let him interfere with my acting dream. Unbeknownst to me, I was auditioning for the part of his wife. Later, I found out that he had played a pivotal role in me landing the part.

Have you ever had one of those life-defining moments, when you felt the world stop and everything hinged on one decision—and in that decision, you knew your life would never be the same? I had that moment immediately, following the second audition. Josh pulled me aside and said, "I'm moving to NYC as soon as we finish this movie, and I won't be coming back. We have to get it filmed in 7 days." I thought, "It's now or never. If it's going to happen, it must happen now." I had no idea why I thought those words. I had no idea what the "it" meant either. I only knew the pull was stronger than anything I had ever felt, and I needed answers. So, I accepted the movie role.

The movie was a very intense, dramatic film about a marriage being torn apart by the accidental death of a couple's son. I intended that for the entire seven days of filming, I would completely immerse myself in my character and her life. Lacking little formal training, I did not realize I was naturally falling into the Method acting technique. I was only following my instincts for my new role.

The movie plot centered around married high school sweethearts who were caught in a tragedy of trauma, loss, and addiction. The lead character, Josh, was guilt-ridden by his own negligence in the death of his son. Grieving their loss, the family unraveled as the husband sank into alcoholism and spousal battery. The finale was the wife (me), murdering her husband and then herself. Not light-hearted scripting! Ultimately, the script would pull up deep, repressed memories, many of which were buried in past lives.

As the movie wrapped, Josh moved to NYC to pursue his acting career, and I returned to my former life as a wife and business owner. However, something was very off. In 7 days, my life felt like it had completely crumbled. What had seemed like "reality" was nothing more than an illusion in my head. As I sat on my porch swing looking across my land, I felt like an alien. I knew nothing, not my husband, not myself. I couldn't understand how a few days could make such a turbulent, abrupt impact on my life. A psychic friend told me that he feared I had suffered a nervous breakdown. The memories of this place were fading fast, and I had no attachment to my former life anymore. A life that felt as solid as concrete only one week before was now utterly unrecognizable. Something had shifted that could not be comprehended. It would be six years before this shift would be fully understood.

Until the movie, I had spent my entire life driven and focused toward achieving goals. My life was very structured and accomplished. Now, I was feeling trapped by the rigidity of it all. And for the first time in my life, I had no direction and no goal to achieve. I felt like a whirlwind. My very structured, conforming husband could not accept all the changes occurring in me. Eight months later, after repeated attempts to pull our marriage back together, my husband, exasperated by it all, left. During one of our final conversations, he said, "I don't know you anymore. Nothing you could say or do would surprise me at this point." These were words coming from a man who had known me since childhood. He was right! I didn't know myself either!

Because I was a seasoned astrologer, I knew there were a few astrological culprits here. First, Uranus, the planet of sudden changes, freedom, and rebellion was cycling through my astrological natal chart** first house of self-identity. Meaning, I was completely reinventing myself into a much truer, authentic, soul-aligned human being. It didn't help that Uranus was also moving through my husband's 7th house of marriage & partnerships, which often indicates marriage upheaval and divorce—if the marriage is unable to embrace the newly changed spouse. Additionally, Pluto, the planet of death-like transformation and new birth, was moving through my 10th house of career and public reputation. With this shift in me, my business in horticulture was phasing out, while my new identity as a spiritual teacher was

---

** An astrological natal chart is a mathematically calculated pie graph that symbolically shows the map of the heavens at the exact moment of birth. Each pie slice is labeled as houses indicating life focal points like marriage, career, health, etc. To the seasoned astrologer, this chart reveals an individual's psychological profile with great precision.

emerging. Yes, a new life was unfolding, with the sudden force and brilliance of a lightning bolt! (Lightening is a symbol of Uranus.)

Several months passed before I could even speak of the film without bursting into tears. I later discovered that the film had revealed past life relationships with Josh. To pinpoint what had happened to me, I voraciously studied everything I could find about soul mates: astrology, numerology, dream interpretation, metaphysical books & psychic readings. I consulted with other astrologers about the strange pull this Josh had on me. I also learned how to do astrology relationship charts, to understand the indescribable energy of soul mates.

With an ending marriage, I needed to make decisions about my home and business. I had always wanted to leave Louisiana since the time my adoptive family took me there from California. Now I had my opportunity! However, my life felt like a spinning tornado that had not yet touched down. I knew it was not the time to make permanent life decisions--yet.

I spent the summer in NYC to attend acting school, but mainly I went to clear my head and make new decisions about my life. I thought, with a new location, I could finally figure my life out. At the Western School of Feng Shui, we had learned the value of travel. As we travel, we leave our comfort zone and habitual patterns. New locations hold no familiarity; thus, they inspire us to grow beyond our normal boundaries.

NYC seemed so HUGE and daunting, but something in me really wanted the challenge to prove myself. With no contacts in the city, I relied on my psychic skills to find an apartment. During my stay in NYC, I was mostly a loner, although I made some friends with my roommates and classmates. I had two very brief visits with Josh; he encouraged me to move to NYC to pursue my acting. Although

I had no answers for my life's direction, NYC, full time, did not feel right, and I knew I was not transforming beyond horticulture into an unpredictable acting career. As with all things in my life, acting was a metaphor for the new career that was being seeded.

Manhattan gave me strength in myself that I had never known. Life in the city challenged me every day. As a psychically sensitive person, the energy of the city was overwhelming, and I found myself struggling to get through each day. I had several teary meltdowns. Through it all, however, I discovered a very free-spirited, independent woman who was now very capable of being outside the security of a relationship. Looking back, my fearless, independent adventure in NYC was one of my proudest accomplishments of this lifetime. Even to this day, recurring visits and dreams to New York continue to strengthen me.

By the end of summer, I knew it was time to return to Louisiana and face my life. After a few very difficult years, I sold my business and home. The death had finally occurred. However, the new life was still a few years from being birthed.

Although I had received my master's in Metaphysics and been privately consulting with clients for years, I still didn't see a spiritual career as a full time, viable option—mainly because I was still in Louisiana. You see, with Louisiana being part of the Bible belt, much of the work I do is frowned upon and is labelled as satanic. As I started to come out of the closet with my spiritual work, many of my old friends and clients shunned me. I'll never forget walking into a dear client's nursery after I sold my business. She snarled, "I hear you're doing psychic readings now." Her attitude was scolding and judgmental. Until then, I had kept my metaphysical studies separate from my horticulture business to avoid the alienation of my clients. However, they only knew a thin veneer of my true self. Now I was quickly outgrowing my old identity, and with my newfound courage, I no longer gave a damn what anyone had to say about it!

For the next six years, Josh & I met over summer and Christmas holidays in Louisiana and New York. We would get together for a day in the summer and the winter. The interaction was never fully consummated or stabilized in relationship. In addition, we never got to know each other or develop any friendship. All that was ever certain between us was that we couldn't stay away from each other. Why we couldn't stay apart, I guess will never be fully understood. During our dates, our unexplainable intense and passionate energy was twisted into bitter power struggles. These struggles found a release in volatile fighting with something like a "draw" at the end of each visit. The exchange was the most bewildering, compelling interaction of my life. These meetings took a toll on me; they left me feeling completely emotionally drained, and afterward, I'd spend weeks revitalizing my lost energy. Often the dread of an upcoming interaction would cause me to refuse to see him.

During these six years, my psychic senses grew exponentially, as a matter of course in relating with him. We never talked on the phone, seldom texted, so on-going communication was nonexistent. I began learning about telepathy, astral travel, and visualization. I came to know that soul mate connections span time and distance. It didn't matter how long we were apart or how little we interacted. Once we were in the same room, the energy between us was electrifying, with even strangers commenting on the intensity.

I had been in long term relationships my entire adult life, but they had never been enough. Once the initial euphoric stages ended, the relationships would taper off into platonic companionship. I'd feel like one of the "walking dead," just going through the motions of my life. After being introduced to this intense soul mate energy with Josh, I knew I wanted my life to be more passionate and adventurous. Lukewarm would no longer cut it. I knew that I would require more from my future relationships.

In between visits with Josh, I loosely dated several other guys, all of which were unusual and unpredictable (another marker of Uranus in the 1st house). Several of these guys were soul mates, and they each gave me contrasting experiences to further refine my relationship dream. In addition to experiencing different people, I also traveled extensively on my own. As a matter of fact, I did almost everything alone in those years! Beyond being a lifetime empath (psychic who feels the energy of people and places), I was finally getting to know MY energy. I was becoming friends with the real me.

With each new guy, I learned further refinement of ME. I knew it was me that had to change to attract the truly connected, enlightened relationship of my dreams. Clients were secretly booking astrology charts and life coaching to help sort out their soul mate relationships. As I continued to learn from my clients and my own relationships, I also made special time to journal daily. I'd write anywhere from 10 minutes to 2 hours, fully engrossed in the visualizations of my future soul mate relationship. Never writing as an intention or goal, I just focused on the details of our dates, our wedding, our marriage, and our shared dreams. I always wrote these little fairytales in present tense. They felt so good that I enjoyed being "there" more than in my everyday life.

Then it happened. What was written on the ethers became manifested reality. On St. Patrick's Day, (my favorite holiday), I was sitting in a coffee shop, writing about my future relationship, when a feeling swept over me, and I thought: "I feel like I already know this guy! He feels so close that I could reach out and touch him!" That evening, dressed in a cute leprechaun costume, I went to listen to a friend's band. At 9:30 pm, I met Matt. There was a difference between Matt and all the other guys. When I looked deep into his eyes, I recognized him, and I could see a future with him. I could see all the fantasies coming true. Abruptly, Matt went to the restroom, and I left to see another band. Matt returned to find that I was gone! He walked outside to find me, but I had already left. Fortunately, I had already given him my contact information. While writing this, I realized this was our "Cinderella moment." Considering my deep involvement with the fairy realm, I was not surprised that my life followed a fairytale theme.

Within a week of knowing each other, we were equally stunned! Statements of "I didn't know people like you existed;" "Where did you come from;" "You're everything I've been looking for;" filled our conversations. However, the first nine months of knowing each other were very hit n' miss. Shakespeare knew what he was talking about when he wrote, "The course of true love never did run smooth." On the surface (and what was being communicated), was that we had opposite desires; truthfully, neither of us were quite a match to our dream relationship. We could see in each other the dream, but we had no idea how to manifest it into reality. Through our erratic interactions, I used the down time to study and grow. My telepathy & clairvoyance skills also grew.

After one of mine & Matt's breaks, a pivotal turning point happened. I officially discovered the world of quantum physics. A dear friend, affectionately known as "China doll," enjoyed deep spiritual discussions with me and offered me the DVD set, "What the Bleep Do We Know? Down the Rabbit Hole."™ I watched these quantum physics DVDs all day long, every day for a month. Each time I watched, multiple layers of reality were revealed to me. My mind was in overdrive!!! I was ecstatic!!!! All the years of study came together and made logical (beyond intuitive) sense. I reflected on Seth's multiple realities, coordinating points and probable selves and fully understood! I knew what Neville Goddard had meant by alternate timelines! Even Abraham-Hicks' light-hearted, simple messages made deeper sense. (Abraham-Hicks is a collection of evolved guides channeled by Esther Hicks.) Scientific facts now supported my intuitive knowledge.

During the collapse of my post-movie reality, no one could explain what had happened. I talked to my therapist, psychics, friends, and healers. No one understood. Now, the answer was clear: I had a quantum shift that put me in a different timeline and reality!

Since my divorce, my life had become a compulsive, passionate journey of living life to the fullest. I spent every day actively refining myself and my relationships. This driving impulse comes from Pluto in my astrological natal chart 7th house of marriage & relationships. You see, Pluto compulsively drives you to dig down deep to explore, heal and understand. The 7th house is a mirror reflection of your self-identity. With all the dots now connecting, it was very natural for me to want to share what I had learned about relating. I began to think about writing this book, first as a soul mate book. Then I expanded the message to include all relationships because the techniques are the same, regardless of relationship type.

As my understanding of quantum physics deepened, I began to contemplate parallel realities, swapping timelines, and shifting identities, as they applied to my life and relationships. I now had scientific proof of the law of attraction; therefore, it made logical sense that I created my reality. I wanted to apply this knowledge to my new relationship with Matt, so I began creating specific energy-molding techniques. The results were amazing! As I talked to both mine and Matt's higher selves, I learned that this was one of our soul purposes in coming together. We deeply desired a connected, expansive relationship, and I was to take what we learned and write a book to help others. Several times, Matt would comment, "Our relationship is an experiment for your book."

Our relationship did become a quantum physics laboratory. As we moved forward, I created many energy exercises to help me shift the energy around the situation. My goal was to shift to a reality that was much more harmonious with our heart desires. I checked in with our higher selves to confirm that my desire was acceptable and ethical. I was told that we each have our own realities that we create moment by moment. I also learned that we absolutely cannot create another person's reality. I knew exactly what I wanted to manifest with Matt, and I knew I could create anything my heart desired. Inevitably, friends began challenging me: "You're working too hard for this relationship," "Leave it alone and trust in the best outcome." Thankfully, these perspectives pushed me into a deeper understanding of the universal quantum laws. Without my sincere, pure desire to enhance relationships, this book would never have made it to completion.

Many people dream of a soul mate or twin flame relationship. Many buy the Hollywood version of relationships, only to become disillusioned when things don't go so smoothly. Time and again, in my life as well as clients' lives, the greater the soul connection, the more tests and difficulties the couple must endure. Don't be discouraged, though; these difficulties aren't meant to last a lifetime. Difficulties occur mostly in the beginning stages when energies are syncing up. If they last the *entire* relationship, there are some unhealthy patterns in place that will need to be shifted, unless the couple choose to live in exhaustive drama.

Abraham-Hicks have been lifetime teachers of mine, and I've always trusted their teachings. However, I was always confused when they'd say things like, "there is no competition" and "it doesn't matter if two people in a relationship want two different things. They BOTH can get what they want." What was the missing puzzle piece to these statements? How could they really be true? How could two different people in a relationship want different things and still BOTH get what they wanted?

I found my answers in the magical world of quantum physics. While this book's teachings are based on quantum physics principles, I choose to communicate these complex principles as simply as possible. Most likely, you are not reading this book to learn more about scientific models. You are reading this book for a practical step-by-step approach to achieving powerful, magical relationship results. We will begin by laying a simple foundation of quantum physics principles. I want to impress that while your shifting relationships may seem magical, they will not be miraculous. Miraculous implies beyond your influence. As you come to understand some basic quantum rules, you will realize why things manifest as they do, and you will feel empowered to design your world according to your desires.

I've created a list to summarize (and simplify) the quantum principles that we will be applying throughout this book.

Quantum Principles:

1. Energy makes up the entire universe.

2. Energy carries a frequency and is magnetized toward other matching frequencies, often called law of attraction.

3. In our 3D-reality, quantum particles seek physical manifestation.

4. Divine has given humans the creative abilities to manifest anything they desire in this dimension.

5. Energy can be tracked by emotional labels.

6. Your thoughts and feelings will reveal how your energy will develop and manifest ahead of time.

7. As you focus on one particle reality, all other possible realities collapse.

8. These quantum laws are universal, unbiased, and apply to everyone. No favoritism!

9. No one can infringe on your reality without your vibrational consent (regardless of how it appears).

10. Your imagination is much more important than you realize.

11. You will need to be a vibrational match to your ideal relationship to ever live it.

12. By maintaining a specific, focused vibration towards your relationship dream, you will begin to see evidence of manifestation.

13. By deliberately harnessing your focus, you will manifest new versions of your entire world.

14. To create quantum shifts, you must be able to suspend your beliefs about reality.

15. Quantum changes can happen at any time! Expect them!

Chapter One
Quantum Physics as a New
Model for Relationships

☆

What you must understand is this: Each of the events in each
of your lives was "once" probable. From a given field of   ☆
action, then, you choose those happenings that will be
physically materialized.   ☆

The Nature of Personal Reality, Jane Roberts

☆   ☆

Quantum Principles Explained

#1 Energy makes up the entire universe.

Broadly, our universe is an electromagnetic field where everything
imaginable potentially exists. The field is likened to a womb
consisting of un-birthed innumerable possible worlds. Each
possible world begins as an electron that represents innumerable
versions of realities and timelines. Once an electron is observed
(with your focus), it collapses into a particle that now has the
potential for manifestation.

You have access to infinite possibilities! Meaning, many different
versions of you & your world exist as potential particles now.
Imagine that!

Figure 1: The Field and Potential Particles

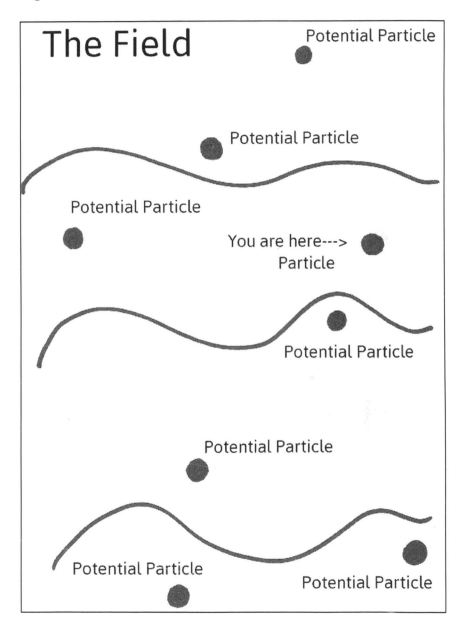

#2 Energy carries a frequency and is magnetized toward other matching frequencies, often called law of attraction.

These floating particles emit specific frequencies; these frequencies create harmony with other particles causing them to gravitate toward each other, better known as the law of attraction.

*For simplicity, we will be interchanging the words vibration, resonance, frequency, & energy signatures throughout the book.

#3 In our 3D-reality, quantum particles seek physical manifestation.

As vibrational resonance is ongoing, we see signs of manifestation everywhere we look. In our Earth-based, 3D-reality, we witness "proof" of physical manifestation. Other dimensions don't necessarily witness the materiality of manifestations. On earth, we interpret energy in physical terms. Here, we confirm manifestation or "reality" through our sensual organs by touching, smelling, tasting, seeing, and hearing. Those of us using our psychic senses, know a thing is "real" even if we can't verify it with our five senses. We can also intuit energy, pre-manifest, and post-manifest, which is called a psychic reading.

#4 Divine has given humans the creative abilities to manifest anything they desire in this dimension.

So how do particles manifest in this reality? To physically, tangibly manifest in your world, one particle must be propelled into manifestation via your intense, thoughtful, emotional focus. Your emotional focus in a single direction creates a vibration that then magnetizes things that match that vibration. Then manifestation occurs.

Manifestations are occurring all around you. It really doesn't matter if you have a goal in mind. You don't need to be a precise person to manifest things. You are constantly emitting a vibrational frequency, which inevitably culminates in manifestation. The question is: will your manifestation be pleasing or displeasing to you? You begin the process of manifestation each time you focus thoughts and feelings towards a given area. If you are not particularly focused, you will manifest all sorts of things, some good, some bad.

#5 Energy can be tracked by emotional labels.

Why are emotions so important? Emotions are the inter-connecting link between you and the field. Your emotions are the etheric cord connecting your solar plexus to your higher self. Your higher self is the soul part of you that is directly linked to God. Your emotions serve as a "telephone line" providing two-way communication between you and your higher self.

Each emotion carries a specific frequency; therefore, a "good" emotion magnetizes more good feeling things. Bad emotions magnetize more bad feeling things. Don't panic and think that every bad thought you think will create a catastrophe in your life! We don't have instant manifestation in 3D-reality. Time is on our side here. The delay between thought and manifestation gives us time to clean nasty thinking up! However, your range of manifestation is strengthened by your more focused, consistent thinking.

In your dream state, you are in the astral realm where you can instantly create things and watch them disappear. This realm is very important in our work because it gives you glimpses of what you are creating. Don't like what you see? Clean up the vibration in your thinking and feelings, before they have a chance to manifest.

#6 Your thoughts and feelings will reveal how your energy will develop and manifest ahead of time.

It is important to understand that the emotional frequency exists *before* the manifestation. People say, "Well, I will get happy when I have something to be happy about." Vibrational resonance doesn't happen that way. You must carry the frequency *before* you see the results. So, if you want love, you must move into that light, sparkly emotion of exhilaration and joy, and then love finds a match with you!

Two of my most striking examples of how emotions reveal upcoming manifestations come from two people, one feeling love, and one feeling hate. Our auric field, which is comprised of frequencies, can be seen by clairvoyants, who are psychics that get visions. The aura reveals the energy signature dominant in a person. I've never fancied myself as an aura reader, but on occasion, certain auric influences stand out to me.

When I am talking to someone who is newly in love, their aura appears sparkly and light pink. There's a glittery atmosphere around the person. I'll never forget talking to a client just before she met someone and right after they began dating. During our first visit, she was excitedly anticipating her lover's arrival. She was draped in a shimmering cloak of joyful expectation. After they began dating, the excitement accelerated to exhilaration. She could not contain all her joy, and she constantly smiled! She was literally high on happiness! I told her, "Remember these moments, because this is the purest energy you will ever feel around this relationship. In the future, you will need to be able to pull from this high energy to improve this relationship or to seek a new relationship." Thus, when a client comes to me seeking love, and their frequency is dark and depressed, I know they aren't quite ready to meet their ideal lover.

On another occasion, a lifelong friend introduced me to her new boyfriend. I immediately got the image of a black, greasy frequency around him. At the time, I wasn't sure what it meant, other than I wanted to get away from the guy. He gave me a very creepy feeling, though he didn't say or do anything to offend me. A year later, this man kidnapped my friend at knifepoint and threatened to kill her. Since that episode, I have noticed that nasty people carry a dark, depressive frequency around them.

Therefore, it's very easy to deduce upcoming manifestations when dealing with consistent emotional patterns. If you dominantly feel good, then good things are on their way. If you dominantly feel bad, then you need to get that vibe cleaned up before you start seeing negative manifestations. Like I said, you have a little wiggle room to play around in the cesspool of negative emotions, but you can't linger there. Oftentimes, when clients are in low places, and they are wanting positive predictions, I know my work is not about the predictions. My work is about helping them get to a more positive vibration and teaching them how to maintain it. For, I know upcoming predictions for a miserable person will be miserable, and I know predictions for a happy person will be happy.

#7 As you focus on one particle reality, all other possible realities collapse.

Thus, the minute you put emotional focus toward a single particle or possibility, all other particles collapse (disappear) from your conscious awareness. This leaves you with one distinct version of reality. Those other particles seem like impossibilities because they are not being witnessed. In personal terms, the collapse of all other particle realities causes you to perceive your life in very limited terms. However, there's good news! If you find your new choice not to your liking, no problem! You can go back and choose another particle through focused, thoughtful, emotion-driven imagination. There are no wrong choices—not ever! You can choose again, and again, and then again.

#8 These quantum laws are universal, unbiased, and apply to everyone. No favoritism!

You have the same opportunities for manifestation as anyone else on this planet. This gift cannot be taken away by your religion, race, gender, body, economic status or any other seeming obstacle. We are all created equal; it is our beliefs that tell us otherwise. People say, "Well, he was born with a silver spoon in his mouth," implying he was born lucky. It doesn't matter what early life conditions were present; you have innumerable opportunities to manifest your dreams.

Self-responsibility is difficult for people to accept. They always want to place blame somewhere else for the lack of happiness in their lives. In my work with clients, the very first thing I ask them is, "Are you ready to give up all ideas of victimhood? You cannot do quantum energy work and believe something outside of you is holding you back." This is an all or nothing subject. You either believe you create it all, or you believe you are a victim of outside people and circumstances.

If your life seems full of unwanted things, then your emotional focus has been dominantly focused on the negative side of vibrational availability. Therefore, each person observes life and then forms an opinion about their observation. As people move through life, they tend to get more jaded because they chronically focus on the negative side of life. Therefore, they get more negative manifestations, i.e. accidents, diseases, broken relationships, etc.

You may offer: "I didn't focus on losing my job, so then why did I lose it?" I'll assume here that you see this as a "bad" thing and proceed with my own questions. Do you complain frequently? Do you notice the negatives of situations and people mostly? Did you secretly wish for more freedom? Sure, you don't have to think about the exact topic to receive a manifestation, but you must be a vibrational match. Now if you answered "No" to all those questions and insisted that you were a high vibrational, positive outlook person, then I'd say this job was not a match to those higher frequencies, and it will be replaced with something much more to your liking, that is if you don't let this loss spiral you downward into negative thinking. Oftentimes, what first looks to be a disaster, eventually turns into a blessing.

Here's another example: Let's say you find yourself in an extremely abusive relationship, and you hear me say, "You are a vibrational match to this person. You create it all." You may ask, "How am I a match to a physically abusive partner? I'm not an abusive person." So, I ask: How did you feel about yourself and relationships before entering this relationship? (Exercise I. will answer this question). What's been your relationship patterns? How does this current abusive partner make you feel? Powerless? Unworthy? Guilty? The negative labels that arise through these questions point to the vibrational match. Thus, attracting anything unwanted points back to a matching vibration in you. If there isn't a match, the law of attraction will not bring you together.

#9 No one can infringe on your reality without your vibrational consent (regardless of how it appears).

The most common excuse I hear is, "I believe someone has put a curse on me," which implies, "I am a victim and have no power." Alright, yes, there are negative people out there who do cast curses. BUT, no one has power over you without your vibrational consent. Curses work on people who are open to negative influences through depression, fear, drugs, alcohol, etc. Curses work on people who feel powerless.

Do you know what "curse" really means? It means someone is sending ill will your way. Well, I'm sure you've witnessed jealousy all your life. You can never stop that, but you can get on top of your game and start deliberately, and actively manifesting your life. Also, you can get clearings for curses and entities as often as you like. Don't let those negative suggestions stop you in your tracks. We're focused on your empowerment.

One night, a mother called in full blown panic! "You must help me! My baby has been crying for days. His stomach is hurting! I took him to the hospital, but they found nothing." The hysterical mother was convinced her in-laws had put a curse on her child, and her hysteria was being picked up by the child. I am not a doctor; therefore, I am not licensed to diagnose or treat anything, but I am a licensed minister, and I do work with God in guiding people. I talked to her about her faith in God, but her faith in evil was stronger than her faith in God. I've seen this a few times with clients. I could not convince them of their own God-given power; powerlessness was all-pervasive in their consciousness. Clinging to their victim mentality, they did not hold the level of consciousness needed to shift their reality.

Another time, a client kept calling every week to talk about finding a job. Finally, after months, she confessed: "4 years ago, I had a terrible spell put on me by a root worker. He's ruined my life. I lost my job, my car, and I'm about to lose my house." I asked her to let me think things over and get back to her. Now, I knew her faith in this spell was overpowering, and I knew she would need some visible evidence of a healing. As she was long distance, I told her to find a charismatic church in her vicinity and tell them her story. I knew they would cast out spirits, and I knew she would probably speak in tongues. This would be the evidence she needed to create in a new way. She found a church, told them her story, and things progressed as I had expected. When she left the church, she felt much lighter and happier in spirit. I will remind you that you cannot take full ownership of manifestation while claiming victimhood in someone else's evil plot—but you can be a partner in their evil intentions.

Take a moment to ask yourself, "Can I release ideas that someone caused my ill fortune? Can I release ideas that someone is blocking my dreams?" If you answered, "yes", then you're ready to deliberately, consciously, start creating your relationships.

#10 Your imagination is much more important than you realize.

As Walt Disney once said, "If you can dream it, you can do it!" Little did he know, his imagination whispered the possibilities of the field. Your imagination is the most powerful tool you own because it directly links you with the Source of Infinite Intelligence and its corresponding field. Your natural desires exist because, on some level, you already know the un-manifested particle exists! How do you know? Your imagination told you so!

#11 You will need to be a vibrational match to your ideal relationship to ever live it.

In this wonderful buffet of opportunities, it follows for every dream, there is a version of you, a personality, who matches that dream. This is a VERY pivotal point in your creative abilities. If you are not the match to the dream, the possibility of manifestation is slim. If you do stumble upon the dream and haven't become a full match, it will swiftly fade, and return to the field, disappearing from your consciousness. Emphatically, I reiterate: you cannot live a dream unless you are a vibrational match to it.

Recently, I sat down with a business owner who was newly in love and launching all kinds of big dreams. She kept telling me, "My boyfriend is so effortless at manifesting. He just believes and tells me to believe. But it all just seems so incredulous!" Upon hearing the word "incredulous", I immediately talked to her about becoming a match to her dreams. I knew, if she didn't swiftly become a match, she could lose it all. Ever heard of lottery winners who lost all their money quickly? They may have been a match to the attraction, but they weren't a match to sustaining the manifestation. This mismatch happened to Matt and me early in our relationship.

In tarot cards, we have a card called the 2 of wands. In this card, we see two wands and a man holding a globe in one hand and a wand in the other, while looking out over the ocean. I love it when this card comes up in client readings! Invariably, this card arises when a client is closing in on a dream. I explain: "Let's imagine you're a farmer sitting on a tractor, plowing a field. There's another version of you sitting in a posh NYC office, overseeing your company. Now the farmer version of you would not be comfortable in NYC any more than your CEO version would feel comfortable on that farm.

You will need to take on the new role, fake it till you make it; until the dream vibration is more comfortable than the old vibration." Same thing goes for relationships. If all you've ever known is rotten, miserable relationships, and you are seeking a heaven-sent soul mate relationship, then you will need to find and carry the vibration that manifests your dream!

For every dream you desire, there is another version of you who matches that reality and is already living it! In this book, you will learn how to find alignment with the version of you who is already living your relationship desires.

#12 By maintaining a specific, focused vibration towards your relationship dream, you will begin to see evidence of manifestation.

The most important requirement of manifesting a relationship is to remain consistent in your focus. You can't be buffeted about by every random thought or emotion. You must hold tight to your goal, regardless of appearances. If you can do this, you will certainly see a relationship manifest.

In this process of focusing, things will start popping all around you. You will see all types of manifestations occurring. These will be your signs that you are lining up your energy toward the things you desire. Early in my own experience, I didn't understand the signs that I was receiving. Like, I'd make a wish, and then signs would start popping up. I took this to mean that my wish was about to come true. Now, I understand that signs are really confirmation that manifestation is slowly occurring. The manifestation is taking shape in the ethers. Let's say you are dreaming of a soul mate relationship. You start seeing all these people who are in soul mate relationships. Everywhere you turn, you see cards, movies, and texts about lovers. You may be like me and think this means your dream lover is about to pop up. I used to think of these signs, "Oh! My dream must be on the way! Why else would I be getting these signs? To torture me?" The universe sends us signs to prove to us that they are listening. The signs we receive, like everything else in this world, are a match to our vibrational frequency. Think of it as your angelic helpers saying, "We heard your request, and here's our proof that we are listening. Keep focusing toward your dream and you will eventually be a match, then we will send you the dream." One little caveat here: if you notice signs and then start to dip vibrationally by slipping into negative emotions (lower vibration), then you've just moved further away from the manifestation. If you maintain joyful expectation while noticing the signs, the energy will continue to coalesce until it "pops" in this reality.

#13 By deliberately harnessing your focus, you will manifest new versions of your entire world.

As you begin focusing on a new vibration, the old particle reality recedes, and you "jump" to a new particle reality. In this new reality, you get to meet new versions of your personality, your body, your life, and your relationships. Therefore, it doesn't really matter if your sister, husband, or friend chooses to change. You don't need them to do one thing! Remember, you are the creator of your reality.

Current relationships are held in place by a set of interactive rules, spoken & unspoken. As you begin shifting, these relationships will be challenged because the old rules will no longer apply. Some relationships will come out the other side, completely altered, while some may dissolve altogether. New people will come into your life matching "the you" that is emerging. As you move through these changes, your dedication to shifting will also be challenged. Remember: change is unsettling and necessary for something better to manifest.

#14 To create quantum shifts, you must be able to suspend your beliefs about reality.

During the filming of the previously mentioned indie movie, I made the commitment to completely immerse myself in my character and her world. In acting terms, this is considered Stanislavsky's Method Technique. On set, I felt my mental stability slipping at times, and perhaps that was when the quantum shift happened. Looking back, I can emphatically confirm that quantum shifts do not require drugs or hallucinogens to achieve results. One only needs to believe and focus to succeed.

During my time in NYC, one of my private acting teachers repeated the mantra:

"To be a great actor, you must be able to suspend your audience's belief in reality."

It is only now that I realize what all those years of exploration and study were teaching me. The art of acting is very much pretending a new life into being. The scenes, the dialogues, the character development very easily blurs the lines between reality and the movie set. What the actor creates from a script blossoms into an entire world before the audience. Hence, the same techniques apply to quantum shifting your life.

From my metaphysical knowledge, I knew that emotion + focus was all that was required to manifest. Thus, I was very concerned that on set creations would carry over into my personal life. Stories abound about actors living similar lives as their characters!

Therefore, without a suspension of belief, you cannot successfully create a new reality. Quite frankly, relationship shifting is easiest when you have time to yourself, like when you are single. When you are in a full-time relationship, you are faced with the other person constantly. It can be quite tricky holding a different focus apart from what is really happening. During client sessions, I offer the potential reality. The doubtful clients continue checking in every few weeks. The "checking" shows that you are not fully married to your vision, and it unravels your work. It's like planting a tulip bulb in a pot and then digging it up every few days. I explain to clients, "I cannot manifest for you; that's your job."

#15 Quantum changes can happen at any time! Expect them!

In the quantum worldview, time is not required to make your changes. But it might take *you* time to make the changes. Let me explain: energy can zoom from one place to another in the blink of an eye. Energy can transform itself instantly. I've witnessed it!

In this new relating style, you are learning all new tools, which may take you some time to master. In the quantum universe, there is no such thing as time. Time is a mental construct we developed in 3D-reality. It only works here. Thus, the length of time it takes you to achieve your goals depends wholly on you and your willingness to shift to the new particle reality. A little secret: currently, the time on our planet has been sped up, and manifestations are happening much more quickly than ever before. That can work in your favor!

I will not tell you that your journey will be light. It will test you. It will require patience. It will require fortitude. You will need to learn a new skill: one of deliberate, consistent, focus. I will promise you this though, the skills you develop from this book can be applied to other areas of your life, like your career, your health, and your personal appearance. These tools will most definitely add to your spiritual growth. Upon learning your new skills, you will come away from this study as a magnificent manifestor, and you will deliberately, consciously create your world. Your old world will have shifted into a brand-new reality.

In summary, the field is where all thought forms exist as potential particles. It's like a thought bank. When someone, like you, focuses on a precise thought or feeling, this focused energy intensifies into one reality, and eventually, materialization appears.

A Particle Relationship

Because life molds the outer world to reflect the inner arrangement of our minds, there is no way of bringing about the outer perfection we seek other than by the transformation of ourselves.

Awakened Imagination, Neville Goddard

Following a rather abrupt fight with then boyfriend, Matt, I witnessed my first quantum physics application. During the fight, we said we never wanted to see each other again. After the argument, I pushed the hurtful words aside and went into my visualization workshop. **I dropped all observance of the reality of our situation and focused on my desire.** I could feel the energetic imprint of Matt's presence all around me, although he refused to talk to me.

Not too long afterwards, I spontaneously received a rather long, heartfelt text from Matt. He said everything I'd ever wanted to hear. He was ready for a committed relationship and wanted to meet. When Matt arrived, he brought me flowers, just as I had seen in the visualizations. In fact, the entire interaction was straight out of my visualizations, with no detail overlooked. Even more shocking, Matt said to me, "I have no idea why I've been away from you for so long." His expression was bewilderment, as though it wasn't him who had said, "I never want to see you again." I immediately recognized this as a new particle reality, but I still wasn't convinced it was a permanent quantum shift. Soon after, I reverted to my old patterns, and things unraveled quickly. It was then that I realized that all new particle worlds would swiftly collapse back into the field unless there were a corresponding shift in personality.

For another month, I continued working on my energy exercises, and I could feel the energetic momentum building. I sensed something major was about to happen that would change everything drastically. And then it happened: Matt's life completely shifted. His old life died, and with it, destructive patterns & people disappeared. A treacherous business partnership completely collapsed.

In true Scorpio phoenix style, the old life burned away to be reborn from the ashes of the old. I am a Scorpio by astrological Sun sign, and Matt's 1st house, or ascendant sign, is Scorpio also. When we invite Scorpio's into our lives, we are preparing for a death/rebirth transformation. We officially began our relationship, but the energy between us was still very unstable. Problems continued to pop up. Realistically, our core wounds were surfacing, and we no longer afforded each other monthly "time-outs" to realign the energy between us.

We fought almost constantly, even though we wanted togetherness deeply. Friends and relatives encouraged a final severing of ties. We broke up. Matt was building a new business; I was without home or career. My life was directionless; I could feel my time in Louisiana was coming to an end. Consequently, my life and finances hit rock bottom, and I was facing bankruptcy. Looking back, I can see how it was the final push into a new life.

By all appearances, Matt & I were finished. However, funny things continued to happen that did not make sense in the "real world." For starters, Matt prolonged replacing his online status to single. He changed his profile picture to a picture he'd taken for me with the sign language for "I love you." I continued to talk to our higher selves and my guides, and I spent an hour daily on energy exercises. During this time, I created the "Field of Dreams" exercise and received a very solid clairvoyant vision. I saw a version of Matt & I newly married and spending our honeymoon in California, which by all real-world appearances *seemed* ridiculous because we were completely estranged. (This by the way, really did come true!)

My psychic skills were moving into new directions. I could feel Matt's energetic presence very strong around me, although there was no contact. It was as though he was always around me. I knew that manifestation occurs only after energy has culminated in a vibrational peak. During one weekend, we made astral love the entire weekend, which he later confirmed. The energy between us was palpable. It was as intense as he had just been in the room with me. I knew the intensity of our combined energies would not still exist if our relationship was over. Do not misunderstand me. There were several times that I asked myself, "Am I crazy? Can I trust invisible guides to lead me in the right direction? Are these guides, mere aspects of my personality? What's the truth here?" I had no idea, but I felt a very deep compulsion to continue forward not only for us, but also for my future relationship book.

After a six-week aborted new beginning in Florida, I drove back to Louisiana, determined to start fresh. On my return, I took a detour through Panama Beach. Matt was heavy on my mind, and I was ready to decide once and for all what to do. I either needed to let go of Matt or commit to this being the relationship of my dreams. I pulled off the highway and typed to my guides. I asked if a future with Matt was possible and what it could be. True to form, my guides advised my future to be whatever I created it to be. They continued to echo the possibility of a relationship with Matt. I was told, "There are no wrong choices here. Each choice comes with a different path. You can be happy with Matt, and you can be happy apart. The choice is up to you." Well, that was very helpful!

Not long after I returned to Louisiana, Matt & I reunited. We rented a little cottage and began working together in his construction business. One year later, we moved to Colorado, married, and launched several businesses. The events that conspired were miraculous, to say the least. My visualizations had centered around us being married, sharing common dreams (though I had no idea what that looked like), and living elsewhere. I saw our marriage as a close, compatible, devoted union of best friends and lovers.

A funny detail I had written in my pre-Matt journaling exercises was grocery shopping with my lover. To this day, grocery shopping is one of Matt's favorite activities to do with me! (He IS a Cancer after all!) Suffice to say, the journaling paid off one-hundred-fold! Things I had merely imagined all came true! Was it easy those first couple of years? No, but the relationship gradually shifted to the vibrational space we both desired.

You may ask, "But what part did Matt have in all of this? What were his desires?" Matt has told me that he knew two weeks after meeting me that we would be married. He's also told me that his dream was very similar to mine; however, he had doubts about the reality of such a dream. He also had a lot of fears. As I did my shifting work, Matt shifted too, and with the updated version of Matt, came a knowing of the dream's reality.

Years later, our relationship has continued to shift to better and better places, as I've shifted into new particle realities. Even now, I look back at our relationship's evolution and glow in the vast richness of the manifestation. I am ecstatic to be a guide for your relationship dreams!

Simultaneous Time

> *That which hath been is now; and that which is*
> *to be hath already been; and God requireth that*
> *which is past.*
>
> *Ecclesiates 3:15*

We love to categorize things, label them and then place them in a box to better understand, and to make life more manageable. However, in so doing, we take the magic & fun out of this world. Time is a human mind construct that overstepped its bounds by making us forget timelessness. All potential particle worlds in all time frames exist *Now.*

The past, present & future are all intermingled into Now. I remember when I first learned this concept. I was stunned, and it took me several years to wrap my mind around the implications. Everything is simultaneously occurring because particles in the field are not limited to any single timeline. You can alter your past by focusing on your future. You can alter your future by focusing on your present. You can alter your present & future by focusing on your past. Furthermore, all timelines are occurring simultaneously; NOW you may be experiencing a lifetime in 200 B.C Egypt, 1808 France, or 2100 Mars. Consequently, it would not be plausible that you are currently being punished for a "past life" crime because *there really is no past*. In addition, it follows that you may pull from talents and wisdom gained in various lifetimes.

Later in the book, we will do the "Re-writing Your Story" exercise to alter your past timeline. This is most effective when you choose to shift a past reality to match you up with the identity of your desire. In other words, by changing "your story", you help yourself create something entirely brand new in the present and future. Much of what keeps patterns locked into place is our habitual replay of our story. By revising our past timelines, we are also able to consciously shift past traumatic episodes.

Psychic Predictions

> *The psychic world... follows a set of laws... With attention and effort, the connection between thoughts, beliefs, and actions can be revealed, and you can create life exactly as you want.*
>
> *Diary of a Psychic, Sonia Choquette*

I went through a long personal struggle for some years. During those years, I turned to spiritual and metaphysical areas for answers. Because this struggle was so personal, it compelled me to push forward in my studies. During those years, I went to many psychics for predictions. Repeatedly, I was assured that my dreams would come true. After many years and readings later, I noticed the dream was still not manifesting.

Honestly, I never gave up on the dream, and I never gave up on my spiritual path. I thought, "Why do you keep seeking outside guidance? You already know the answers that you seek." Eventually, I stopped going outside of myself for most of my answers. Through meditation and automatic writing, I learned to open a direct channel to my higher self and guides. The information I received was amazingly accurate. I continued to refine my writing and began using this guidance in my client's readings; we moved from predictions to soul guidance readings. I also encouraged clients to trust their own inner guidance. With quantum physics, I came to understand that ALL potentials existed. In life coaching and shamanism, I spotlighted my clients' clear desires and helped guide them toward those particle realities. My mission was to open my clients' possibilities and then guide them toward manifestation.

Still, I wanted to understand why some predictions came true and others did not. First, let me say, psychics are not necessarily magical beings (arguably some are), they are simply people who are very adept at reading energy. Think of cartoon characters with thought bubbles above their heads. Each person has a multitude of bubbles, which are potential realities, around their auras. A skilled psychic can read these potentials and convey their interpretation to the client. *Just because the possibility exists, does not mean it will ever manifest. The client must be a vibrational match to witness the manifestation.*

In addition, there's a catch to psychic readers: the psychic will only be able to pick up the potential *they vibrationally match.* For example, you could have an amazing potential reality hovering around you, like a windfall of money, but your psychic is a depressive, jaded sort. That psychic may not pick up your amazing possibility. They will instead tap into your negative potentials. Why? Because they do not match the frequency of amazing potentials!

Today, I was talking to a client about attracting her ideal love relationship. She said she'd always had bad luck in love. I kept seeing something from her childhood that was murky and holding her back from her dream. I told her this would need to be healed and released before she would line up with her ideal relationship. She shared that when she was 19-years-old, a psychic randomly approached her and said, "You will never be happy in love. You will have bad luck in your love life." As a young, impressionable girl, she bought that statement as fact and carried it all through her life until today, 22 years later, when she met me. As I was staring at my beautiful, raven-haired client, her story reminded me of Snow White. I advised, "This is your medicine. Re-write this story and cast yourself as Snow White, the beautiful, young maiden who was full of life. See that psychic as the Wicked Witch who, green with envy, wanted to steal your joy and beauty. Complete the story with the curse being lifted--because today—it was." Later, we will talk more about the magic of revising your story.

Now, I'm not sure if the cursing, negative woman was really a psychic or just a jealous woman who wanted to cause harm to a young, beautiful girl. It doesn't matter who the messenger really was. The message did its damage because this young girl held a matching frequency to the message. Her beliefs insured that she would go on to attract events and people to prove the prediction. A different girl may have heard that psychic's words and shouted: "You're a crazy old lady! Speak your evil somewhere else! Your words won't stick to me!" In which case, she wouldn't be a matching frequency, and she wouldn't go on to create proof of such a curse.

Although I believe everyone creates their individual realities, I do not remove myself from the responsibility of my impact on others. Anytime we take a profession of guiding people, we are placed in a powerful position that must be used with the purest of intentions. Many people place great faith in psychics' impressions, and I hate to say that there are unscrupulous psychics, just as there are unscrupulous people in all walks of life. When a person is psychically gifted, they should exercise great care and integrity when disseminating information.

Aside from our "Snow White" example, predictions are more dependably accurate when the predictions are short-term probabilities. Why? With time, things change. Timelines alter as people shift. New choices set up new possible outcomes. With quantum shifting, the future is even more malleable. It can be read today and be completely shifted out by tomorrow. That is the beauty of simultaneous time! Nothing is destiny!

An example of creation-in-motion comes from a client who asked me to read the Akashic records of her troubled teenage son. The Akashic record library contains universal records. Each being's thoughts, actions, purposes, and lessons are contained within the records. They show the possibilities of all timelines: past, present, and future. However, the details can shift (even past ones), which will completely shift the records. Again, energy is not static. There is nothing "set in stone." When I went into the library to see the boy's records, I saw him in his early twenties getting into lots of trouble; guns and gangs came up. I shared this with the mother who cried, "You just broke my heart!" I replied, "I must be honest with you, but you're learning this early enough to help him shift this timeline." After the phone call, I checked his astrology chart. I found this boy to have a brilliant mind, and he embodies the warrior archetype. Thus, he will always be compelled to fight. The trick will be to fight for a worthy, noble cause, not a destructive one.

You and You

Man's chief delusion is his conviction that there are causes other than his own state of consciousness. All that befalls a man happens as a result of his state of consciousness.

The Power of Awareness, Neville Goddard

Invariably, some people may question: "Is *Mystical Empress Magical Relationships* a method of taking away another person's free will?" If you truly understand the law of attraction, the field, and particles, you will know this is impossible. Simply put, **you create every version of every person in your reality**. You give every person their words and their actions. In truth, the only person you can ever control is you because you are the creator & director of all that you experience. Why? Because every relationship is between you and you. Your vibrational offering creates the relationship and person you experience.

I'm sure you've heard that corny adage: "You must love yourself before you can love anyone else." You literally must love yourself before you can love another because you will only create what you already are. If you don't love you, then you will emit that vibration, and you will attract others who feel same. Thus, it behooves you to begin shifting to the particle personality that *you love and enjoy.*

Just as you create the people in your life, so do other people create versions of you in their lives. Your will cannot be forced on another person. They are equally creating their separate reality, just as you are. Thus, even when you are in the same house, conflicting desires still don't negate you or your partner's desires. You both can create what you each desire in your respective particle realities. As I sit here editing this book, I'm witnessing our soul mate cat, Sir Gawain. He's actively focusing on spending his nights outside.

He's sitting poised in the direction of the door trying to collapse the door's molecules so that he may run free. My desire for him to be safe and healthy indoors is as powerful as his desire to roam free in the neighborhood. Briefly, I pondered his desire and concluded that he can create an outdoor life in *his reality*, which I do not have to experience, while I create his exclusive indoor life in *my reality*. I know this can get real hairy, and it may take some time to wrap your mind around. For now, just know: there are as many versions of reality as there are people (and animals) on this planet.

Now, let's look at a relationship between people. Let's say you currently desire a relationship with a certain person. In your relationship creations, there must be a matching version of both you and the other person to manifest your desired relationship. If you both have a corresponding match, then you will come together in a relationship. However, if there is no match, no relationship will manifest. Going one step further, if you align with another potential particle, by way of shifting you, that same person may become a match to your vibrational offering. If there are no versions, this person will fade from your love life, and you may go on to create your relationship desire with another. Later, we will discuss how to know if a certain person exists in any of your particle realities.

If another person's words & actions are not agreeable to you, then you must shift you. You cannot change them, not ever. It's not a matter of imposing your will on them by being a bigger bully. In this universe, it's an impossibility to force something on someone--unless they are already a vibrational match. However, as you change, the new you will call a matching version of them (if one exists). As you begin making changes in you, one of two things will result: this version of them will leave with a new replacement version who matches the new you; or if they've served their purpose in your life under the soul agreement, the new you will see them leave your life.

I was asked by a teenager, "How do I stop taking what people say and do so personally?" Firstly, most people are completely caught up in their own worlds, and they aren't necessarily aware of you. Sure, they may react to you, but it's not necessarily from a conscious place. Next, you created this version of them in your life, for your own purposes. For example, a rude person may be reflecting your lack of boundaries and unwillingness to stick up for yourself.

So why in the world is relationship even necessary when you're basically having a relationship with yourself? Life hands us mirrors because it is easier to see clearly when the object is outside of self. We come to this planet like lab scientists who are constantly digging and sorting through data in search of desirable blends. Initially, we incarnate not understanding our creative abilities, then through multiple lifetime experiences, we evolve to understand that we create it all. As our paradigm shifts, we begin to deliberately mold energy toward desired results. At this stage of our evolution, we have fulfilled our human life intention.

You may be thinking: "That's too much work! I don't want to work that hard for any relationship." My reply: the work is on *you*. If you don't want to work that hard on shifting yourself to a better version of you-that is your prerogative. You will meet the versions of people who match you right where you currently stand. So, if you haven't been real excited about your past relationships, you may want to give this a try. No matter what kinds of relationships you have, there's always room for improvement. One thing is certain: for every inch of effort you give, you will move to a better place in your relationship manifestations.

If your desire is to control, harm or manipulate another being, your intention will create a vibrational frequency that the law of attraction will swiftly match. You will magnetize other situations and people of similar intent. This is what the law of karma is about: what you sow, you will reap. The universe does not punish, it only serves up a matching vibration.

For every relationship dream you desire, the field requires a version of you who embodies that desire. This is a book about shifting *you* to be the version of the person who is already living their relationship dreams. If you were already this version, you would already be living your dreams. We often fail to realize that our dreams require something of us. They require a certain set of beliefs, attitudes, and actions.

Dreams will often take time to manifest, but not because the universe insists on a specified time span. We've already learned that time is simultaneous, so things do not require "time". The time involved is the "time" it takes you to shift to the corresponding personality who matches the dream. This shift can occur in the blink of an eye or over the course of a lifetime. It all depends on you. In this book, I will offer you techniques & methods that have worked for me. These methods were refined during several years and condensed to aid you in swift manifestation.

You already know what the current version of the story gets you. You cannot expect external changes without corresponding internal changes.

Chapter Two
Discovery

☆

☆

☆

He who knows others is learned;
He who knows himself is wise.

☆

☆

Tao te Ching, Lao-tzu

☆

This section is labeled "Discovery" because we are merely collecting data here. Do not judge anything you learn about yourself. Be curious. This section is here to help you objectively investigate your past and current life experiences. It does not predetermine your future. I've included it because an examination of lifelong patterns will help you to understand why you've created the life you've experienced. Now that you have a new understanding of different versions of self, you may choose to shift into more beneficial versions for greater relationship satisfaction. In later chapters, we will discuss techniques for shifting.

Seeds Planted Eventually Germinate

Examining Early Parent/Child Relationships

When we have a dream in sight, we seldom want to take time to look at our past and how it has affected our now (and potentially our future). The earliest relationship bonds were formed with our primary caregivers, usually our parents. Our sibling relationships play a less significant role in our relationship style, unless our siblings played a long-term caregiver role. The parental relationship dynamic, created between our parents and us, provides our initial models for future relating. We watch our parents relate to each other, and we watch them relate to us. These early bonds will continue to infiltrate all our relationships until we highlight, heal & shift them.

Many of us have witnessed very unhealthy parental relationship dynamics, thus most of us will likely leave our childhood environment with fears concerning relationships. Fear always creates blocks. We may have experienced abuse, abandonment, neglect, or rejection. As we mature and develop into adult relationships, these patterns will continue to manifest in our relationships, even when we've sworn never to repeat our parents' mistakes! We will give and receive similar behavior as our early experiences are already imprinted upon us. These early experiences imprinted us with certain vibrational frequencies which will attract others who will fulfill the same dynamic. Unless we work to understand and shift these vibrations, we will most certainly develop relationships that continue the patterns.

Particularly, soul mate relationships provide intense experiences (often painfully), involving the very core issue we are grappling to acknowledge and shift. As soul mate relationships seem destined in importance to us, we will stick with them longer than other relationships, and in effect, give ourselves repeated chances to grow past our original core wounds.

An example is your mother favoring your older sister. You were repeatedly told, "If only you were more like your sister." Through this experience, you felt rejection, competition, and abandonment. As you grew into a teenager, you were constantly competing with your sister for boyfriends. As you reached adulthood, your relationship pattern consisted of a triangle involving you, a desired lover, and another person who supplied competition.

If you were to live this situation, you may wonder, "Why would I create this in my world? If I didn't like it as a child, then why would I want it as an adult?" Simply put, we don't choose by our words; we choose by our habitual thought-feeling patterns, which carry a vibrational frequency. Habitual thinking sets an energetic tone that sends a magnetizing signal out into the ethers. This tone attracts similar vibrations to it. Whether you like something or not, it does not matter. What matters in the creation of anything is how much attention you give to it. The more thought + emotion you apply to a person or thing, the more likelihood of creating it in your life. I have witnessed people who, ensnared in an old vibration, compulsively go to the very people who dredge up the old patterns and completely dismiss those who would engage healthy relationships.

Those old patterns from our childhood continue to reappear because early childhood imprinting carries the most weight of all our learning stages. Why? Because this is a time in which most development and growth occurs.

Ancestral Lineage

Although I was adopted, I intermittently continued contact with my biological family and explored my Native American family lineage. Through shamanic journeys, I explored my ancestral DNA. I discovered many repeating patterns. Ironically, these ancestral patterns carried over to my adoptive family tree. How could I leave my biological family, only to find same issues in the adoptive family that raised me? In reviewing astrology charts, I am continuously amazed by lessons that repeat in multiple biological family charts and adoptive family charts. This confirms that we choose soul lessons, and circumstances beyond our conscious control do not erase those intentions.

DNA is much more than physically inherited material. DNA is an indicator of established vibrational patterning. It indicates energetic belief systems within a closed system. Most people think if it's in their DNA, they're stuck with the outcome. DNA, as with all energy, can be shifted and expanded. In our soul state, we make co-creative agreements with others to fulfill specific growth experiences. Through vibrational resonance, we are magnetically attracted into these families that match our original intentions. Our family of origin sets the stage for the core lifetime issues we choose to master. Sometimes it seems like we are thrust into situations haphazardly. I've heard people say, "I don't belong to this family. Somebody made a mistake to put me here." Nope, no mistake, just vibrational matching. No-one and no-thing can be in our experience without a vibrational match. Additionally, the astrology chart reveals that soul birth intentions begin manifesting early in our life experience. It's like we hit the ground running as soon as we are born!

As you come to understand the power of your focusing mechanism, which is your mind, you can shift to access the infiniteness of your DNA. This shift sets you on a completely different channel of brain wiring, which then unfolds a different life. Additionally, your shift affects all those aspects interacting with you and around you. This means YOU affect the shifting of your family lineage as it relates to you. Time is simultaneous; thus, your shift affects past, present, & future ancestors. Additionally, shifting your DNA helps you to evolve beyond 3D duality awareness and into 5D expansiveness.

Many of the clients that I attract are here to bring healing and awareness to their family lineage. A metaphor I use in my work is to ask my client to see a long strand of light bulbs. These bulbs represent past, present and future generations in their family lineage. Every bulb is out, except for one. The lit bulb represents my client. As my client works toward healing and growth, they give every other bulb an opportunity to "come on". I often use DNA recoding as well as clearing old ancestral lessons to help my clients untangle from these old vibrational ties. Much energy is released to be used in more productive ways. Moreover, their family relationships shift, and their past and future ancestors are positively affected.

Neural Net Communities

Our brains are designed with electromagnetic pathways called neural nets. These neural nets are like small communities that link memories with beliefs. Neural net communities are electrically activated when specific thoughts and feelings activate beliefs. The electrical currents then stimulate the hypothalamic gland to inject the body with chemicals that induce specific emotional highs & lows. Thus, your body becomes trained to know what thought or feeling will induce its chemical high. This habitual cause & effect pattern is what makes it so difficult to change destructive patterns. The body craves specific chemicals, which in turn provokes the mind to summon the thoughts/feelings. We become addicted to these thought/feeling patterns. We then create external circumstances to validate the thought/feeling as a true belief. As we believe, we create, and so the cycle continues. It is crucial to realize that neural nets are recharged with *every reaction that confirms its core belief*. Additionally, medications, alcohol, caffeine, nicotine, sugar and mood-altering drugs (plant and chemical-based), can create an artificial release of these hormones. Hence, addictions set in and make changing patterns difficult to achieve.

While working with a client who had recurring illogical fears that she couldn't shake, I explained, "Your body gets a high each time you think that thought. Thus, like a junkie, you will need to go through withdrawal and change your thinking habit." In my life, I've had a similar recurring paranoia from prior PTSD. Of course, it was irrational, meaning it was deep subconscious patterning, but nothing I did could shake it. Years of therapy didn't even phase it! Then one day I found myself going down that old familiar rabbit hole, and I stopped myself. I thought, "Ok, you already know where this train of thought takes you-- down a bottomless pit. If you will stop the thought, right here and now, you can bring yourself back to the present moment of your adult, rational self." As I repeated this new habit, it grew, and the post-traumatic belief lost its hold on me. Just as a junkie believes that one tiny injection of heroine won't be a problem, you cannot afford to entertain these trauma-based thoughts for a minute, or you will get trapped in the downward spiral again. With quantum shifting, these old, ingrained beliefs can be shifted, but it takes repeated consistent effort.

New neural nets are built on thought processes changing and then affirmative reactions to these changes. To dissolve an old neural net and belief pattern, we will need to stop reacting to thoughts and feelings that seduce us into recharging the old. By directing more focus and reaction to new, positive beliefs, we enable the growth of new neural nets. With this shift in focus, old neural nets eventually disintegrate. We will still get our chemical release, but only now it will involve positive thinking.

Although core beliefs originate in early childhood familial dynamics, we seldom challenge them; we just assume they are the truth. One of the most powerful statements I ever read was, "Just because you believe it, doesn't make it true." As we never stop to question our beliefs, we merely continue to confirm their validity by creating new affirming scenarios. We are convinced by what the world continues to show us. Why? Evidence proves the early belief. Thus, it is easy to be seduced by external reality. However, you create the evidence because it matches what you already believe to be true. See, there is absolutely no way to get away from yourself!

One day I was talking with a client about her evasive husband, who she felt was surely about to divorce her. We began to explore her childhood, and her father figure. She remarked, "My dad acted like this; my uncle acted like this. So, I just always expected to be treated this way by my husband." What happened here? Two things: 1) she was drawn to the man who matched a similar frequency as her male relatives, 2) she continued to summon that behavior from this man via her own expectations (frequency).

I often use Shakespeare's "All the world is a stage" metaphor when talking to clients. Quite literally, we are each the directors, producers, and actors in our own play. Through the vibration of our thoughts, feelings, and beliefs, we cast the characters, write their scripts, and set the plots. So why do we take our plays so literally? If we could see the world as plastic, we would automatically understand the fluidity of reality. If we could stop thinking "It's so REAL," (implying a fixed nature), we would move through the dramas of our lives much quicker, and eventually, stop creating 90% of them!

Watch your thoughts and feelings as they bubble up. Watch people and situations pop up to push you into a reaction. Each time this occurs, reel your mind back in and resist the urge to react. As you shift into new patterns, you make the decision to shift out of the old, familiar way of doing things. The old system will fight for its survival. These continuous provocations will tempt you to react in old ways. If you observe these and simply acknowledge them, they will eventually fall away and stop occurring. In building a new set of beliefs, based on new choices and new thought patterns, you are creating brand new neural nets. Your new frequency will magnetize new matches of people, places, and things into your life, which will confirm your new reality. Eventually, you will look back on what you thought to be true and hysterically laugh at the illusion of it all—just as the enlightened masters did!

Abstract Art Journaling

We are now ready to discover our relationship patterns through art & journaling. I've found that combining writing with art is a very useful tool in expressing undiscovered subconscious material. The process of writing and drawing/painting/coloring unites both the logical and the creative hemispheres of the brain. This means that you're using more of your brain than usual, revealing more useful information. Much of our inner truth comes through when the mind is uncensored and allowed to express spontaneously.

Please commit an hour or more to exercises #1 and #5. Choose only 1 topic per exercise per day. While simple to complete, these exercises are deeply revealing and can be very exhaustive, as your subconscious releases material that may take some time to process. All sorts of emotions may wash over you, so please take your time, drink LOTS of water, and spend time in sunlight and nature to ground you. I emphasize water because it is a conductor of energy, and we are moving a lot of energy!

For these discovery exercises, you will need a drawing pad (preferably 18x24" so you're not cramped on space), crayons, markers or colored pencils. Choose many colors to reveal the varying shades of your emotions. Commit this pad to be your ongoing art journal. Without expectation or judgment, allow yourself to express whatever comes up freely.

Exercise I. Old Neural Net Pathways (see figure 2 for a beginning example)

Begin at the center of your page: write the word that best describes the relationship topic you are reviewing. Examples: Love, Trust, Sex. Instead, you may write the word that best describes the type of relationship you are reviewing: Mother, Husband, Best Friend. After writing the focal word on the center of the page, draw a curvy shape enclosing your word, and then draw an outline around the shape. This enclosure serves as the heart of this drawing. Choose two happy, positive colors: one for the inside of the enclosure and one for the outline of the enclosure.

Never touching this central enclosure, begin writing all limiting, negative descriptive labels & brief phrases that spontaneously surface about your central, enclosed focal word. Encapsulate these negative labels within jagged, harsh outlines everywhere on the page—DO NOT touch your central, enclosed focal word. Do not evaluate or censure these labels as they come up. They come from the purity of your subconscious. Example: If your focal point word is "LOVE," negative labels that emerge may include: fear, unworthiness, betrayal, lies, deceit, infidelity, scary, loss, abandonment, and trapped.

After enclosing the negative words, draw connecting lines (bridges) to each shape on the page—DO NOT touch the central, enclosed focal word. Next, draw zig-zag, dried up tails on each negative shape. These tails denote the "break" from the central focal word. If you mistakenly draw a connecting line to the central word, it acts as a subconscious flag of your unwillingness to drop that connecting belief. IF you do this, my strongest suggestion is to remove the page and begin anew. Choose a dark, "ugly" color to symbolize "dead" neural net and color all negative shapes, tails, bridges, and words. Color a bar across each negative label to denote "No." Shade light enough so that you may still see the negative word underneath.

If you do not get this exercise completed in one sitting, do your best to get it done as soon as possible. I advise you not to make this an "incomplete art project" hidden in a closet. This exercise provokes powerful change, and if left hanging, could impede your progress. As you complete this exercise, a door closes and awaits a new door to open. (In Chapter 3, we will create the new doorway.) Label your completed drawing: "Old Neural Net". Be sure to drink plenty of water and rest. You just did a tremendous amount of work--great job!

You may repeat this exercise with any troublesome relationship areas. This exercise is designed to help you shift through the previous relationship limiting beliefs. From this moment forward, pay attention to seeming evidence that tries to "prove" these old beliefs. Yes, the old "proof" will try to cajole and intimidate you into reaction. It needs its chemical fix! Just shoo it away like a fly!

Reflection:

Sit with your completed picture. Allow yourself to understand & accept that every negative label is a belief you currently hold about relationships. These beliefs create the "proof" in your relationships. If you cannot accept your part in creating the unwanted, you will not be able to permit yourself to create the wanted. In addition, some of these labels will feel particularly charged. These intensely charged dynamos reach back to unresolved core wounds.

Figure 2 Old Neural Net Pathways

Exercise II. Key Relationship Pictures

Choose key relationships such as parents' marriage, relationship with parents, siblings, first love, best friend, extended family, co-worker, or marriage. Example: "My Parents' Relationship." Without thinking about it, allow your inner child to draw whatever image that comes to mind. It could be a symbol of rotten fruit. The picture could show stick people with hearts all around. Any image is valid. Remember, this is your subconscious revealing its deepest truth. As you draw, do not stop to evaluate. Keep going until you are finished. Then, before you color your picture, you may take a moment to look. Go on to color the image because you are marrying the brain's hemispheres in agreement. Coloring will lock this new revelation into conscious awareness.

Reflection:

Repeated journaling and doodling have been proven to calm the mind and reveal solutions to problems.

Exercise III. Journaling Reflections

Another very useful tool is writing your thoughts in a journal. As the previous exercises have undoubtedly unlocked memories & beliefs, you will want to explore your emerging feelings on these subjects. Also, exploring revealed patterns will help you to understand them better and replace them. Without this exercise of your written conscious acknowledgement, you may block the catalyst of change concurrent with these new understandings. In addition, your journal will serve as a progressive confirmation of the shifting you complete. Feel free to color and draw around your writing, as this too, adds power to your words.

Reflection:

Do you feel like you are peeling back layers of an onion? Stay calm and hydrated as you are doing a lot of work. The act of writing is one of the most powerful, magical manifesting tools that you can use.

Chapter Three
Attracting New Relationships

That we might not even have noticed…
☆ *Except for that faint quiver of wonder* ☆
We loved ☆
And the closest we've come to explaining why ☆
☆ *Is because it was you*
And because it was I ☆

Venus Trines at Midnight, Linda Goodman

As human beings, our core impulse is to Love. Love comes with no guarantees, no backup plans, and no nets to catch us when we fall. Loving is often one of the most frightening things we will ever do, very much like dying. We enter love relationships with many subconscious, preconditioned responses. As the sparkle fades, these old patterns surface, and we swiftly recede into the shadows. I heard this last night when my client called. She said, "We were doing so great! Then poof! He was gone! I have no idea what happened!" Fear is what happened. Humans want and need love more than anything, but it scares them to death!

As in the neural nets, repeated life experiences can harden us into reaffirming our erroneous beliefs. These beliefs keep us trapped in the past and away from our joy; they keep us bound to fear and suffering. Fear and love cannot coexist because they are energetic opposites. When you feel fear, worry, hate, doubt, and anger, you are not feeling love in that moment. Fortunately for us, emotions are fluid and ever-changing, like water.

Anything you desire to be, do, or have, is already an alternate reality enjoying its existence. Through the following techniques, you can line up with your dream version and call it into your conscious awareness now. First, you must become a vibrational match to that particle version of you. The cleanest cut is to fully, unabashedly accept your 100% creation of every relationship interaction you've ever lived. If you continue to think *people have done something to you,* you will continue to act as though you are a powerless victim, which is *your creation.* So please full-heartedly, accept your responsibility in creating your previous relationship dynamics.

Who Have You Been?

By completing the discovery exercises, you now have a pretty good idea of who you are in relationships. You also have a pretty good idea of who you are not. Through the process of elimination, you can conclude that whatever you desire requires a completely different version of you than you have been in the past, and anything before this moment is past. If you were already the desired version, you would already be living your desired relationship. By fully accepting your creative responsibility in previous relationship dynamics, you are holding the key that unlocks the door to future optimal relationships. Congratulations! You have now stepped through the doorway to manifesting your desired relationship.

Early on, I learned relationships were the greatest classroom for self-discovery. Most people go through life playing victim to others' actions & words, never suspecting they created "other." I also learned through my research, revisions, and shifts that I could create anything I wanted, with one catch: the manifestation would always be a PERFECT match to my current personality. Let me explain. Ever heard that old saying: "Be careful what you wish for, you might just get it"? Whoever you are in the current reality, creates a vibration that you emanate into the universe. This vibration will draw a perfect match. Ever heard of people who get fat surgically removed, only to gain it all back very quickly? Why does this happen? While they were a match to removing the fat, they had not shifted to the skinny self-identity. They continued to focus on their overweight self until it re-manifested.

Likewise, you may attract the most amazing life partner in the world, BUT if you are not the version who matches an amazing relationship, you will see that person vanish from your life. I was once told of a woman who made a relationship checklist. She thoroughly defined what she wanted, without putting focus on the unwanted. However, when she attracted her new mate, she got all that she wanted plus some very unwanted characteristics. Logical deduction may cause you to think: "Well, she should've covered her bases by listing the things she didn't want." If we focus on the unwanted, then we draw it to us. As previously discussed, the field only requires emotional focus toward a particle to propel it into reality. This story reveals she was not the personality who created a loving, healthy, harmonious relationship. The personality that attracted this relationship had limiting beliefs about the potential for her dream relationship.

If you've been single for a while, you may be dominantly vibrating "single"; thus, you will not attract a commitment. Do you see yourself as a single person? When you look at other couples, do you envy them for finding their life partner? These feelings indicate that you're still carrying the identity of non-relationship. I can remember watching affectionate couples on the subways in NY. At first, when I wasn't a match, I felt sad that I didn't have someone special. In fact, I'd never been in a publicly affectionate relationship. My mates were always too embarrassed to cuddle openly. During my single years, I learned how to use these symbols as tools to help me visualize my desires. I made a point to celebrate every single loving couple because in my heart *I knew my day was coming!* And it did! I'll never forget the first time Matt stopped talking to a friend to give me a kiss when I arrived. I felt so special that he'd publicly show his love. Believe me, these things can happen to you too!

Environment as a Metaphor

As with all things, homes carry vibrational imprints. Based on your vibration, you will subconsciously choose a matching vibration in your home. Your address, your decoration, your organization, and your home's "flow" will all be a perfect match to your vibration.

With my Feng Shui training, I teach clients to see their homes as gigantic vision boards with symbols that reveal their intentions and beliefs. I enter the home reading the symbols. Based on the client's desires, I then make recommendations for furniture arrangement, colors, textures, shapes, smells, organization & artwork. In this way, the client has a pro-active, visual approach to the manifestation of their dreams.

The things encountered daily speak volumes about our beliefs and intentions. I once had a single client who called me for help in manifesting her ideal relationship. As I walked through her home, I saw the repeating pattern of "single." Her choice in artwork invariably displayed strong, single women. In her bathroom, I noticed one hand towel & one bath towel. On the back patio, she had a single chair overlooking the flower garden. Her master bedroom, the primary intimacy symbol, was most revealing. Stuffed dolls decorated the room. The pillows were stacked to one side of the bed, and stoically standing beside the bed, was a single nightstand. Repeatedly, I saw my client's truest belief, which seemed to be screaming at me: "I AM SINGLE!" Unknowingly, she had affirmed her current truth, which was exactly opposite of her desire. Well, that's all fine and dandy if you want to make a statement about factual conditions, which we often do, to our own detriment. If your real desire is opposite your reality, you will want to let your fact-based reality fade away in favor of new affirmative symbols, (and stories).

Completing my environmental analysis, I gave my client recommendations for removing relationship blockers and replacing them with brand new relationship enhancers. The very act of making the change often shifts the client's identity. Then the daily, repeated confrontation with relationship symbols helps reinforce the new neural net. Shortly thereafter, she had a vision of her soul mate. It took her a few more years of dating, but she did finally meet and marry him.

Exercise IV. Does Your Environment Agree with You?

The next time you're away from home, return wearing new glasses. You don't wear glasses? Well, pretend that you do. As you approach your home, I'd like for you to see it in a new way; see things as a first-time visitor would notice them. Driving up to your house, what do you feel? Does this home look inviting? Would you be inspired to stop here and get to know the owner? Pay special attention to the landscaping and the front entrance. Are they inviting?

As you walk through the front door, notice sounds, smells, and visual cues. Does anything feel threatening, like say, a thorny cactus houseplant? Stroll through the house looking at art objects. Is there a theme? Does this theme match your desire for relationship?

Pay special attention to your master bedroom. Does it look like a single person lives there? Are things arranged to suit one person in your bed? Is the room full of clutter that pushes new energy out?

Are there dolls all over the bed, implying unresolved childhood issues? Is the bed surrounded by electronics? Take these questions and form some of your own. Use your new "glasses" to really review what your home is saying about your desires.

Reflection:

Was your house a match to your new dream or was it still confirming your old reality? Make some changes, and see what happens.

Exercise V. New Neural Net Pathways (see figure 3 for a beginning example)

Now you are ready to create a completely new neural net from your old neural net in Exercise I. By interjecting positive beliefs around your original focal word, you begin to create a new neural net. Do not try to do this exercise before completing the negative version in Exercise I. This picture picks up where the last one left off by replacing all the negative beliefs with positive, new beliefs. Through continued confirmation of these new beliefs, this new neural net will help you shift beyond your current reality.

Begin at the center of your page: write the word that best describes the relationship topic you are reviewing (return to Exercise I., Old Neural Net Pathways.) Examples: Love, Trust, Sex. Instead, you may write the word that best describes the type of relationship you are reviewing: Mother, Husband, Best Friend. After writing the focal word on the center of the page, draw a curvy shape enclosing your word, and then draw an outline around the shape. This enclosure serves as the heart of this drawing. Choose two happy, positive colors: one for the inside of the enclosure and one for the outline of the enclosure. You will repeat these colors over the entire drawing.

Without touching your enclosure, begin writing all positive descriptive labels & brief phrases that spontaneously surface about your central, enclosed focal word. Encapsulate these positive labels within flowing, curving outlines everywhere on the page. Do not evaluate or censure these labels as they come up. They come from the purity of your subconscious. Example: If your focal point word is "LOVE," positive labels that emerge may include: joy, security, commitment, monogamy, trust, and passion, or "you're everything to me."

After writing the positive words, draw connecting lines (bridges) to each shape on the page INCLUDING the central focal word. Draw as many bridges to your focal word as possible. These bridges imply an acceptance of these new beliefs about your focal word. Next, using the original two colors of your focal word, choose one for the bridges and one for the curvy shapes & positive words. Shade light enough so that you can still see the positive wording underneath.

Be sure to allot enough time to finish the drawing in one sitting because you are channeling tremendous energy in this new neural net. Do not lose your momentum! I do not advise waiting for later completion. This exercise provokes powerful change, and if left hanging, could impede your progress. With the completion of your drawing, you have just walked through a new door and a new reality. As before, please drink plenty of water and allow for adequate rest. Label this drawing: New Neural Net.

Anytime the old neural net beliefs try to pop into your reality, observe and replace the thoughts with the new neural net beliefs.

Reflection:

Do you feel relief? Anticipation? Excitement?

Figure 3 New Neural Net Pathways

Hop Scotch Time

Events and objects are not absolute, remember, but plastic.
Events can be changed both before and after their occurrences.

Seth Speaks, Jane Roberts

Previously, we briefly discussed simultaneous time. Time construction is only a "law" in our world. Other dimensions and beings do not use time. We originally created time as a way of sequentially measuring events. However, sequential events are an illusion because time does not flow in one direction, and single timelines do not exist. Time mythology tries to limit energy flowing in all directions. It can't be done.

There are certain illusions that humans, as a mass consciousness, agreed upon. Time is one of them. Separation is another. Through countless generations of agreement, these erroneous beliefs grew until they were the only acceptable explanations of reality. The problem with this mass time agreement is that it eliminates the ability to shift into new particle realities. We are so hypnotized by believing in one reality that we haven't been able to awaken to alternate realities.

Furthermore, as you are actively shifting your reality, you cannot focus on the way it has been AND the way you want it to become. By trying to do this, you are trying to straddle two different timelines and particle realities. This work will require you to commit to a single path, no matter what "reality" shoves in your face. Am I asking you to be delusional? No, not in a psychotic sense, but perhaps, to the people around you, you may appear delusional. I'd advise you to keep this work to yourself.

I was coaching a client on her love life, and she was best friends with a well-meaning, astrology novice. Every time I'd give my client homework, she'd discuss it with her friend. Her friend would recite astrological transits and progressions that would plant disbelief in our work. Astrological transits and progressions are cycles that indicate <u>possible</u> upcoming events. My client began our sessions by quoting her friend's predictions. Exasperated, I told her, "Your friend is operating from a linear set of laws. I'm taking you quantum where everything is possible." As a professional astrologer, I am very aware of current cycles; however, I do not use them to stifle my creativity and block my freedom. At the beginning of my spiritual journey, a friend handed me <u>Autobiography of a Yogi</u>. I read that the more evolved a person becomes, the less their astrological natal chart will match them. I have remembered those words and always used them as a check on my astrology knowledge. Later, we will look at some broad astrological cycles that correspond to significant life changes. I use astrology mostly as a tool for unmasking psychological patterning, relationship dynamics and soul intentions. The only time I specifically use astrology for timing is when I'm setting important dates for new ventures. For, the more engaged to a clock and a calendar you are, the less open to quantum shifting you will be. Sure, you most likely have a job and kids that require a certain schedule, but wherever possible, pull back from clocks and dates. Don't add time where it doesn't need to be.

Since we have access to varying timelines, this means we can land at any point on a timeline. Consider a man who is approaching his 45th birthday. Throughout his life, his body has appeared to go through a maturation process and then as maturity peaked, his body began to gradually decline. This example shows a single timeline with a sequential evolution of events. Now, let's reflect on multiple timelines. On another timeline, this man may be in a body that is actively growing younger. Still, another timeline may reveal this man's body never saw a decline. His body may have never passed the youthful appearance of a 20 something-year-old. Yes, these are all possible realities. As we are learning to shift particle realities in relationships, we can also shift particle realities in body and health situations. Remember: physical matter is made up of energy, which is highly moldable. Nothing is fixed in stone.

Quantum Physics Interference of the Past

The past existed in multitudinous ways. You only experienced one probable past. By changing this past in your mind now, in your present, you can change not only its nature, but its effect, and not only upon yourself, but upon others.

Seth Speaks, Jane Roberts

We've all wished that we could change things about our past. Well, I am here to tell you that you do hold that power. Don't believe me? By writing the past as you would've preferred it to be and believing the new story, it automatically, energetically shifts your present and future. You are tapping into the field and choosing a new particle. In writing this new story, you re-write yourself and your life story. Who would you BE if your past had happened the way you wished? Your entire perception of YOU changes. Even traumatic events that seem locked into history can fall away as if they never happened. So how does this work? Simple. You shift particle realities where life DID happen the way you wanted.

I can hear your immediate reaction: "What about the real world? By imagining something, it doesn't necessarily make it true! People will think I'm crazy!" First, you must give up clinging to this reality as the one and only truth. It is only true because your continued focus has made it so. There are multiple realities just waiting for you to pluck them from the field. Why cling to a reality that is not pleasing to you? Also, your imagination brought your current reality into being, so why can't your imagination create a new one? Finally, I agree, people will think you're crazy! So-- don't tell them what you're doing! It's a funny thing though, as you quietly go about molding your reality, those same people will change to meet your new identity anyway! They never need to know they changed!

A young millennial came to me about her unending string of bad luck. For starters, I noticed how she carried the vibration of fear and powerlessness. As I explored more, I could feel the energy of rape all over her aura. I suspected she had already been accosted and the vibration had not been healed. She had entity attachments that were drawn to her tattered aura. I said, "I do not want to scare you, but I must warn you that the vibration of sexual abuse is all over you. You must get this energy cleaned up quickly, so you do not attract any more trauma to yourself." Unfortunately, this girl took recreational drugs and lived as a vagabond. She spent most of her time in a woozy, unconscious state, which she interpreted as "spiritual." Although she confirmed prior sexual abuse, she didn't take my advice.

While I'm talking about recreational drugs, I need to add a precautionary note. The work in this book requires you to be fully conscious and locked into your body's awareness. You don't need any substance to achieve what I'm teaching. Many people are dabbling in plant and chemical substances, thinking they need these things to achieve altered states and enlightenment. The common argument is, "Well, the shamans take it, so I can too."

Wrong. Tribal shamans are raised in cultures that respect plants and proper, healthful usage. They are not gluttons for "highs." These chemicals are taken sparingly as part of sacred, spiritual ceremonies.

The danger of being under a substance's influence is that it opens you to all kinds of psychic energies, entities, and abuses. It's like nobody's home with the door wide open. When things attach themselves to you, as with the millennial, you are a match to many nasty things coming your way. Most often the people who "stay under the influence" are also people who are hiding from a great deal in life. They carry unhealed traumas and turn to substances to numb the pain. What they end up creating is more pain.

Additionally, your subconscious acts as a protective gate that guards your ego against traumatic memories, until the personality is ready to process them. By engaging in substances, we may accidentally blow that protective gate open, unleashing all kinds of memories way before their healthy timing. A young, psychotherapist client once mentioned that she gave suffering PTSD clients LSD at summer music festivals. I was horrified!!!!! I shuddered to think of traumatized young adults being exposed to more unpredictable, potentially traumatic experiences.

While the exercises in this book can alter your reality, they do so without taking you away from your body. You have complete control of your consciousness at any time. You don't lose your consciousness or your healthy boundaries. You are safe. Realize, Neptune is the planet of spirituality, drugs, deception, illusion, dreams, music, film, and entities. There's a fine line between healthy spiritual exploration and destructive self-deception. Folks who abuse substances also have strong Neptunian influences in their astrology charts.

The following exercises will give you firsthand experience in shifting timelines. These are mind & reality bending exercises! Yes, they are as magical as they sound. Do not be surprised when key players and events shift overnight without any conscious awareness of the shift. (Don't try to explain their shifts to them; they will not understand.) I've had absent lovers return as totally changed people! Have fun!

Exercise VI. Re-Writing Your Story

In your journal, begin writing the perfect version of your past from a first-person perspective. You may start at any point, such as childhood, divorce, or career change. Write the story in present tense as your most powerful manifestation occurs in the present now. I find that the further back on the timeline I go, the more creative power I hold in shifting adult events.

Every detail about yourself, your personal relationships, and your life should come through a different lens. If you were a shy person, write yourself to be out-going and confident! Write about how you interacted with others, and how they reacted to you. Fill in as many emotionally colored details as possible. DO NOT add any negative details.

This simple, yet extremely profound exercise will change your entire life, as you begin to remember this story as the *true story*. Are you practicing denial? Indeed, but only for a brief wrinkle in time. Soon, you will start to notice your life magically shifting. Besides, what is healthier, continuing to dredge painful memories OR constructively creating a healthy new future launching pad? Just don't share this with your family & friends, for they will argue the "truth" of your past, unless and until they shift. You will most likely choose to stop discussing past events so that you may disentangle from that old vibration.

This exercise has remarkable repercussions for current relationship dynamics. As you re-write a past relationship to a healthier, happier dynamic, it energetically shifts the current dynamics into something more productive and positive. Always remember, if you slip back into an old you, you will also flip your relationships back to the old patterns. Thus, all changes begin and end with you. Until this new personality is firmly rooted as your dominant vibration, you run the risk of reverting to an old particle reality.

Reflection:

How does it feel to be this new person? How does this new personality react to life events? Is this new person a logical match to your relationship dream?

Whom Do You Seek?

At this point, you've undoubtedly stirred many relationship memories. Each relationship you ever experienced added to your list of wanted & unwanted traits. The more relationships you encountered, the more opportunities were given to clarify your desires. NEVER be ashamed of your specific relationship desires. You came by way of these desires through your uniquely clarifying experiences.

Exercise VII. Designing Your Ideal Partner

In list form, write out what traits, personality, social status, habits, appearance, values, & beliefs you desire in your mate. Be as verbose as you wish! Sky's the limit! Generally, however, it is best not to be too limiting in the physical appearance, such as a 5'9 blonde, blue-eyed female with a perfect hourglass figure, as Miss Right could appear at 5'1, brunette, green-eyed, with a petite frame. If you are ONLY looking for a blondie, you may ignore your soul mate or Miss Blondie may appear but not have the rest of the package you seek. Only you will know what your top priorities are in a mate, and yes, you can attract whatever you want, given you are a corresponding match.

I've been warned that in making this list, one must be exacting in their details; otherwise, that one thing that was left off will be the most unwanted thing that arrives as part of the package. I get a good chuckle at this superstitious way of manifesting. You WILL manifest what you match. If you fear that unwanted "thing" or otherwise hold tremendous resistance toward it, then yes, you will most likely draw it to you. If you choose to write down what you don't want, then write these descriptions in healthy, wanted terms, not "I know I don't want a lazy bum." Rather than writing that statement, which calls it into your experience, you may restate it as, "My mate is a disciplined, conscientious worker who manifests plenty of money."

Also, if you attract Mr. Right but he has one fatal flaw, and you think, "I must kick him to the curb! He's not perfect!" *HOLD UP!* First, shift YOU, find the matching chord that attracted that flaw and shift it. Then, watch him shift out the door, or he'll shift to a new matching version. Of course, you can accept Mr. Right with his flaw. In all instances, it is your creation and your choice.

Reflection:

Do you believe a person this wonderful really exists? (They do!)

Exercise VIII. The Field of Dreams

The field holds all possibilities. It does not dictate desire or push you into specific choices. The field is neutral as far as your personal desires go. The field's only desire is one of loving continual expansion. In this exercise, you will create an open channel for the field to impress you with the particle that matches your desire. Through prayer, meditation, or intention, you may ask the field to impress your imagination with a representation of your ideal relationship. Ask, "I am requesting a vision from Divine of my ideal relationship." In this open, allowing space, you may receive pictures, words, sounds, or smells. As a visual person, I generally receive visions from the field.

Please do not censor the information coming from the field. Immediately dismiss any urge your rational mind makes to denounce the information. By allowing the information to flow freely, you are creating a bridge between your imagination and the field. And yes, the information is valid. If something shows up, that is not what you desire, gently release the information and start over. Sometimes, it takes switching the "channel" to something more appealing.

As you start to feel elation, joy, and hopefulness, know that you are tuning into a probable reality of the desired relationship that is *already in existence*. Stay in this space for as long as you can hold your focus. From this exercise, retain as many details & emotional responses through journaling your impressions. You just received a glimpse of the "future" of what is already waiting for you. I highly recommend returning to this vision as often as possible, to create a bridging vibration between present and future realities.

Reflection:

After this exercise, do you feel like you know this person? (You do!) It is true that the one you are seeking is already seeking you too!

Exercise IX. You, the Movie Director

To make this exercise potently effective, complete it in 2 parts: The first part involves writing a perfect scene from a moment in time in your ideal relationship. This scene is like a movie trailer, including weather, location, costume, dialogue, characters (you & your partner), action, time of day/season/year. Go into the scene, feel it fully and talk from a first-person vantage point (hint: even more powerful if done by using information from exercise VIII). This is the exercise that I was writing daily during the creation of my relationship. The second part of the exercise is optional; you can draw a picture of your perfect scene.

Example: The sun is setting on the turquoise ocean; little sparkles of diamonds crest on each wave. The breeze is nice and warm. I'm walking down the beach holding hands with my lover. I'm wearing a gauzy white sundress, and I feel so beautiful & feminine. He's wearing khaki cargo shorts without a shirt. I look at his sculpted chest and arms, and I feel like I'm swooning. We walk to some clustered rocks and share a kiss. Unexpectedly, he looks deeply into my eyes and whispers, "You're my everything. Will you marry me?"

After the written version is completed, you may now draw the scene. The picture itself is not as important as the feelings the drawing evokes in you. Be creative & colorful! While this exercise can be done at any time of the day, extra power is summoned when done just before going to bed or napping because in sleep-state, your subconscious takes over manifesting.

Repeat this exercise for different events. I recommend doing it as often as possible. With each repeat, you are building the vibrational bridge to the matching version of reality.

Reflection:

Does this scene feel more real than reality? (In this moment of focused attention, it is). Writing a new scene for a minimum of 10 minutes a day will create many miracles in your life!

Am I Getting Close?

Fortunately, there are definite sign posts to let you know how close you are to your dream. These signposts all involve feelings. If you shun feelings, you will be missing out on one of God's greatest communication tools concerning YOU. Realize happy relationships are based on feelings. The heart does not always speak in words.

First, let's review what your emotions mean, so you can connect what you're feeling and consequently attracting. Negative, resistant, limiting, fearful, and angry emotions push your dreams away and attract unwanted things into your life. These emotions may include hate, anger, fear, depression, powerlessness, guilt, sorrow, or jealousy, among others. Neutral emotions like disappointment, frustration, or cynicism just keep you on the fence and unmoving. While positive emotions like hope, expectation, faith, love, passion, optimism, and joy, mean you're closing in on your dream, plus other delightful manifestations! A very simple way to shift negative emotions is to write a gratitude list. Genuine gratitude is a high vibration, which draws wanted things to you. In their book, *Ask and It Is Given*, Abraham-Hicks offers a wonderful emotional guidance scale that lets you know exactly where you are in proximity to your manifestations. I highly recommend it!

As you do exercises V-IX, a curious thing will happen. You will start to feel lighter, happier and increasingly expectant of good things coming your way—and they will! Expectation is a high vibration of electromagnetic attraction. As you continue to repeat Exercise IX, you will begin to invoke feelings of elation. You will perceive that you are already with your mate. You will catch yourself forgetting that you haven't begun the relationship yet. Also, you will feel so joyful in your reveries that the actual manifestation ceases to matter. You're having a relationship before the person shows up! Once you begin to feel the presence of this stranger in your daily life, KNOW that you will be meeting your mate very soon. The vibrational signature is a precursor to the manifestation.

During my single years, I was writing these movie scripts daily. Each new date brought new revisions to my scripts. On the day 1 met Matt, I felt a "click" during my writing. I just knew he was right around the corner, and he was, by about 5 hours! Within my field of dreams visions, I saw a dark-haired male, who looked exactly like Matt. Although I never tried to pin down my lover's appearance, I was glad to get a visual image of him. One of my male Indian clients asked, "Tell me what my lover looks like! What color hair does she have? What race is she?" I responded, "If I let you pin me down to physical details, you will be running through the streets looking for exactly someone who matches my description. You will miss other people on your path. Trust she is coming and drop the need for details. Let yourself be enchanted!"

By learning to tune into energy, you will always know what is coming to you. You will become your own personal psychic! If you find that you are uncomfortable with the energy surrounding you, spend time cleaning up and clearing out the unwanted vibration. Remember: You create it all. Thus, you always vibrationally choose what is coming to you.

Chapter Four
Harmonizing Existing Relationships

But let there be spaces in your togetherness and let the winds of the heavens dance between you. Love one another but make not a bond of love: let it rather be a moving sea between the shores of your souls.

The Prophet, Khalil Gibran

Romantic Relationships

I believe we can all agree that new, fresh relationships are much easier to navigate than long-term existing relationships. Why is that? As a relationship continues, we start noticing our partner's little flaws. As we notice more and more, the flaws begin to grow until they seem insurmountable. What happened? We may ask, "Has my partner been hiding his true colors from me?"

I've been told that one cannot trust the "realness" of a person until after the 6th month of dating because that is the *magic* month for revealing true personalities. I disagree. Prolonged interaction reveals YOU. Simply put: you're on your best behavior in the initial stages of dating; you're admiring your creation and keeping it positive. After the initial euphoria begins to fade, you flip back into old patterns and simultaneously start to resist what you evoke from the individual… then things begin to unravel. The longer we know a person, the less likely we are to focus on their good traits. If we focus on the unwanted in ANY individual, we are sure to breed more unwanted along with a scornful contempt from the person.

Remember what you witness is merely a reflection of your vibration. Have you ever had a friend who adamantly disagreed with your opinion of someone? Better yet, try a sibling who perceives a different version of a parent. You wonder, "How in the world do they not see what I see?" We witness our matching vibration.

Incidentally, people's powerful expectations can find a matching vibration in you and summon a reaction. I once had a mail lady that always seemed to summon bizarre rude behavior from me. As I'd part from her, I'd think, "What in the world just happened to me? Why did I react like that?" She quite possibly held a fearful vibration, and her vibration matched anger in me. As a severely abused child, I carried a lot of fear and anger. These frequencies always found a match in school yard bullies. You see, it works both ways.

Infidelity and Open Relationships

Affairs happen when a person has reached their maximum resistance toward their partner. They see greener pastures on the horizon and choose a new mate. However, a peak in resistance is the *worst* time to seek a new mate. Why? Because your vibrational matching is full of yucky stuff! You cannot hope to attract anything beyond your vibration. Sure, the new lover seems to be everything the spouse was not, but give it time. Your vibrational pull will bear witness, and you will eventually manifest very similar traits in the new love. You can't get away from yourself! Of course, if you do the work to shift the old beliefs and patterns, you will have a much better chance of the new lover being different, but most people don't take the time to do that. And surprise! When you shift to a new identity, you will attract something new from your old mate too, and you may find yourself falling in love all over again!

Let's say you decide to have an affair on your wife. You're sick of her nagging you and taking you for granted. You notice that hot new secretary at the firm and begin flirting with her. The relationship begins as an emotional dumping ground where you list your wife's intolerable traits. Then the relationship proceeds to the physical level. You think this woman is your soul mate! She's everything you've ever imagined a woman to be. But you forget, you're still carrying that old vibration from your marriage. In time, your new mate will start to evoke the old familiar emotions and thoughts you had about your wife. Why would she do such a thing? Because your vibration is what is creating her.

Currently, there's a growing trend of open relationships where each partner openly agrees to sexual partnering with others outside their primary relationship. If each person genuinely feels inspired to follow this path joyfully, then these couples can achieve happiness in open arrangements. However, if the couple is seeking multiple partners to avoid affairs and divorce, the value is lost. Neither open relationship nor monogamy will "cure" the underlying vibrational pattern. You must get you lined up before you will be happy in any type of relationship. Once you are lined up, your sexual desires may very well change too.

A note about monogamy: I see clients all the time who are suffering from frequently cheating lovers. Often, they feel something is wrong with them to make their lover wander. They think if they just "stick it out," their lover will change. It is true that some people prefer one lover at a time, and some people prefer multiple lovers. Some people are sex addicts. Ironically, many monogamous people partner with non-monogamous people, which is an indicator of resistant beliefs in <u>both partners</u>. Rather than cleaning up their own relationship vibration, they settle for less, hoping to change the partner. If you are one of these people on either end, you may work these relationship exercises to shift to a new identity. During the process, your mate will either shift or not. If they do not, you will go on to attract your desired relationship. Invariably, clients who are "plagued" by unfaithful lovers always carry strong frequencies of distrust, betrayal, rejection, and abandonment. Without cleaning up the vibration, how can they hope to attract anything better?

Platonic Relationships

We can see that we deliberately choose our lovers and friends, but what about those seemingly "fated" relationships? Relationships with family, co-workers, and neighbors can raise our ire because we feel the most powerless to change them. You may have an adult daughter who curses you every time you call her. Your co-worker may constantly sabotage your work. Your neighbor may hold loud weeknight parties that keep you awake. In these instances, it is natural to feel powerless and victimized initially. While justified, these emotions take you away from the powerful position of creating your life, on your terms.

Long-term relationships seldom consistently attract positive vibrational matches. On the light side, we get mad at each other, have arguments and make up. On the heavy side, we simply cannot stand to be in the presence of the other person. More commonly, the vibrational thread bounces between wanted and unwanted ranges as you observe one another. So, whose fault is it that the observed person is disagreeable to you? If you create your reality, wouldn't the responsibility fall on your shoulders? It is your observation that reveals your vibrational match. If you are observing unwanted personality traits, it is because you have a matching vibration that creates their behavior.

If you shift your focus, then the disagreeable person will come around only during peaceful times or bar peaceful moments, they will completely disappear. Mothers tend to have the most difficulty with law of attraction matching. They want so much to be involved in their adult child's life that they will endure all kinds of negative exchanges to remain in contact. By shifting self, first, the universe will bring you together when the exchange is harmonious. This may be less frequently than you desire, and you will need to ask yourself, "Is togetherness more important than my wellbeing?" If the answer is "yes," then don't change a thing and just keep banging it out together! If "no" is the answer, you owe it to yourself and your relationship to shift yourself through the exercises in this book. Be curious to see which version of your adult child reappears.

So, a girl might ask, "What do I do when my friend is going through a turbulent time? Shouldn't I be there for her?" First and foremost, you owe it to yourself to stay in a good vibrational space. How does that help your friend? If you get down in the hole with her, then you're just two equally miserable people with no solutions. If you can offer guidance from a positive, connected space, then you are of value. As I am mostly working with suffering people, I cannot allow myself to get stuck in their problems. I remind myself that every person has their own soul path, and I have no way of knowing their exact path. Things that appear painful to me, might be the lesson they needed to grow and heal. While I feel empathy, I do not allow myself to take on another's energy. I offer the clearest guidance and spiritual shifting that I can summon and release the person to their angels. I recognize that I am not the Savior; I am a tool for clarity. If healing is to take place, it is between the Creator and the human. Once the session or interaction is completed, I expect the best for the person and release the episode. If I were to obsess over their problems and worry about the outcome, it would not be a healthy situation for me. Some think it's cold to not willingly sacrifice their joy for another's suffering. What the unhealthy see as cold, I see as healthy boundaries.

Remember: there are as many different versions of people as there are realities. Each version has its corresponding past, present, & future. You can create harmony in ANY relationship. It is your choice what you create, and it all depends on your shifting focus. The other person doesn't have to lift one finger, but they unknowingly do. They don't even have to know you are shifting the relationship, but they often change, too. IF there isn't a corresponding version of a person to match your improved vibrational focus, they will no longer be a major player in your life. They may even completely fade from your life. At the very least, your shifted focus will no longer observe their unwanted behavior—and you will have peace. As you continue to rescue a person, you don't get more peace, you get more drama. It can be no other way. Also, as your focus shifts, they can no longer do that annoying thing in your reality. This doesn't mean someone else may not observe their unwanted behavior, but you will be immune to it.

Shifting Discordant Relationships

Each time we witness anything unwanted, it is our job to recognize it as unwanted and then immediately shift ourselves to match what is wanted. What do most of us do? We start complaining about the unwanted, mistakenly thinking that if we complain long enough, things will change. Guess what? It doesn't change, it grows! If a person does something we don't like, all our focus typically goes toward the other person in hopes of changing them! We cannot evoke in another what we haven't become in ourselves.

Many clients have been involved in relationships for years. They've seen zero improvement in 5, 10, 24 years. It is very difficult to convince the individual to take their focus off the lover, family member, boss, etc. They waste their energy and power by focusing purely on the offending party. If they can focus on shifting self, the rest will take care of itself. They will see a shift in the relationship.

I anticipate that the previous exercises in the Discovery section helped you come to the realization and acceptance that you are 100% in charge of creating your relationship. If you're not happy in your relationship, then it's time to roll up your sleeves and get to work on yourself. Interestingly, as you begin shifting you, miraculous things begin to happen. The other person starts changing without any nagging coming from you. Things that you thought would never happen—do happen. Other possibilities exist too. As you change, you may decide to separate from this person. During your shifting, it will be impossible to predict what will happen. Astonished clients call me exclaiming, "I started working on me, and the most miraculous changes happened in my relationships!!!!"

A father of an adult alcoholic daughter came to see me. He was at the end of his rope, after years of bailing his daughter out. Exasperated and hopeless, he worried for his granddaughter because he knew how unreliable his daughter was. Understandably, he felt very obligated to help them. However, his daughter was an adult, with her own path and choices. He had spent years pleading with her to change, but the problem had only gotten worse. He didn't understand that his focus on the problem only added fuel to the fire. I explained, "Your daughter has her own path, and she's learning lessons along that path that add to her soul's overall growth. You can never understand those lessons. Your granddaughter was a tough little bugger because she knew what her mother's life looked like, and she still chose to come in as her daughter anyway! In the same vein as your daughter, your granddaughter also has lessons she wants to learn. Children create their realities just as adults do. Do not mistake this child as powerless. She is not, and she may end up creating a different path in which she doesn't stay with her mother."

As the father, he carried tremendous influence with his adult daughter. Remember, parental relationships are our first lessons in relating, and so, parental beliefs carry extra weight in a child's lifetime conditioning. A parent's expectations are extremely influential in a child. There is a very strong psychic cord bond between parent and child which carries the parent's expectations psychically to the child. Because of this intense psychic energy, a parent will always serve their child best by expecting the best for them. A parent's fear, worry, and doubt only negatively influence their child.

We've learned that no one can be in our lives without a vibrational matching. So where did this story begin? Dad was raised by an alcoholic father, who was also raised by an alcoholic uncle. The addiction vibration ran very strong throughout the family. Dad was a teetotaler, but the vibration remained, and his daughter carried the DNA. His powerless, chaotic childhood was never shifted, and his daughter resurrected those feelings.

When a person finds themselves in the position of this father, being worried and terrified of an outcome, it becomes much harder to shift the focus. The mind wants to keep playing worst-case scenarios. Remember, the neural net is offering a chemical fix in exchange for the fear. Shifting is crucial to be free of torment and make positive changes in the situation. Parents and grandparents have some of the most difficult shifting to do because a) they feel responsible to rescue their children and grandchildren b) their children's actions can literally be life-threatening.

Working together, we shifted the father's DNA, which would automatically shift his daughter's DNA. After our spiritual shifting sessions, his identity began to shift. He repeatedly worked the following exercise, "Creating New Worlds," which set the tone for a completely different vibrational field around himself and his relationship with his daughter. Moreover, the shift in vibration also changed everything else in his life.

What happened? Ten months went by without a word from his daughter. One day, out of the blue, he received a call from his daughter who had been sober for nine months. Her life had radically changed—without any words or overt action from her father. She was going to the gym, eating healthy, and living in a cute little cottage. She had a good stable job, and she was very active in her community. What of the granddaughter? She started making straight A's in school, was taking piano lessons and playing on a softball team.

Notice how the father did not push for interaction. He just let things be as he did his shifting work. His vibration began shifting past the old dynamic and into his new identity. The "old" daughter did not contact him either; he heard from the "new" daughter in her newly shifted reality. If he had pushed for an exchange, he may have unraveled his shifting and flipped back into the old dynamic.

If you have a troublesome relationship, do not push for interactions; do your shifting work, and then allow the universe to do your scheduling for you. The universe will match your vibration every time. If you are in a good mood, and the other person is feeling negative, you will not have an exchange. The quantum attraction will not be there to be in each other's presence. If you do what most people do, however, and push through the "off feeling" and meet because it was prescheduled anyway, you may have a discordant exchange. With personal interactions, you may wish to be much more fluid in your scheduling, so that you can access the energy vibe before the meeting.

When a client calls during a rocky separation or break in relationship, I always encourage them to back away from the person and do their shifting work. Usually, they panic and want to rush to the person, which will only make matters worse. During my own courtship, I took "off times" from Matt to work on me and to do the exercises presented in this book. Each little break was used to shift me to a new, better place. Then when we reunited, our relationship had shifted to a much more harmonious place.

I think I'm most baffled by people who continue toxic relationships, especially when family is involved, without ever shifting or separating—even when the relationship is highly destructive to them. Fortunately, for our father/daughter duo, their relationship had grown so toxic, that he could no longer prop her up. He had to make the self-loving decision to separate. In many other instances, I've witnessed adult children who were earlier betrayed by their mothers in favor of an abusive spouse. Rather than shifting OR staying away, the adult children maintained the relationship quietly, while carrying bitterness and unresolved wounds. I do not believe any of us were born destined for destructive relationships. So yes, learning the exercises in this book will restore your power in all relationships and then you can make the decision of how you wish to proceed.

A client came to me in tears. She had followed new age studies for years, but they didn't seem to work for her. As we talked, the onion peeled itself. Her despair led back to her mother, and what her mother had failed to do. My client had never married, never had a family, had led a miserable, single, reclusive life, and according to her, it was all her mother's fault! I asked, "Do you still interact with your mother?" She said, "Yes, and it is very upsetting to be around her. She's never loved me!" I asked, "With all this bitterness in your heart, do you think your mother enjoys your interactions?" She quietly looked down at the table. I went on, "When you feel negative feelings about someone, and you interact with them, they feel that negativity coming at them as a psychic attack. Unless they're telepathic, they won't be sure what the negative vibe is about, but they will still feel it. Until or unless you can clean up your vibration about this relationship, you and mom will both be better off spending time apart."

We grow up in a society that teaches a mother's unconditional love as the Mother Mary archetype loved Jesus. Mother Mary was the perfection of motherly love. Sure, we can strive toward that perfection, but we are still human and flawed. There are other faces of mother that other cultures recognize: Devouring, Abandoning, and Rejecting are some of the others. If you've ever watched nature, you will see each of these mother masks play out.

I tell my adult clients to strive toward seeing their parents as human beings with flaws. They aren't godly figures; they make mistakes. They have normal emotions just as we do. After the real human parent is revealed, then I recommend shifting the relationship dynamic toward friendship and away from parental authority figure. Why do I say this? Most adult children flip into a childlike role when their parents are around, and then normal interaction can swiftly turn up old power struggles. Compare the statement: "I think curtains in your living room would look nice." Coming from a friend, it feels neutral because you know it is just an opinion. Coming from your mother, who always seemed to ridicule your choices, it feels more like a criticism, and you grow defensive. A friend is someone you choose to spend time around because you enjoy their company. There's no "ought" or "should" in the equation, and it makes for a much purer, harmonious interaction. You don't carry baggage around, typically, with a friend. Our next exercise will give you an opportunity to try different relationship roles. See which one fits you best.

Make no mistake, in your shifting; you are not taking responsibility away from the other person. They have their own reasons for their actions. You cannot change them. That is their choice. All you can do is change your reality. The beauty of relationships is that they hold a magic mirror that says, "These are your trouble spots. I will play this role until you figure out how you create your reality." The more painful the interaction, the more we are motivated to grow from the experience.

I guarantee you that NO MATTER what your relationship looks like now, it can change to something better—if you choose to drop the blame game and shift yourself instead. Granted, "better" may mean a complete separation, but often better comes from a more harmonious exchange between people. I've seen people shift and notice the other person is fading out of their life, and so they immediately revert to the old dynamic to continue the relationship. I encourage you to move through the fear toward a healthy version relationship. Take the risk, you owe it to yourself.

Exercise X. Creating New Worlds

For this next exercise, you will start with the current "problem" in your relationship. You already know what "it" is, so now decide what the opposite would look like. Let's say you've always dreamed of a marriage that is mutually helpful, respectful, thoughtful, and loving. At this very moment you look up as your husband storms in the house from baseball practice. He throws all his clothes off in the middle of the room, tosses his gear on the bedroom floor, jumps in the shower and then leaves to go hang out with his friends. You think, "Nope, married the wrong man."

From the problem, you will begin designing a movie script of your relationship without the problem. Please remember: this is not a script about problem solving; you're not looking for "solutions." Your ONLY job is to decide what is wanted and begin imagining that version of your relationship. Your co-star can be your partner, family member, friend, co-worker, or even a stranger, whichever feels most comfortable and easy to create. Be cognizant, though, that you're creating worlds in this exercise, and by doing the scene with another partner, you are setting the vibrational tone for a new partner to enter your life!

Create your perfect scene with all the props and characters in place, as follows for this example: Today is my birthday, and my husband has really surprised me! He sat on the bed this morning and said, "I've really been thinking about what a wonderful person you are. I realize where I've fallen short, and I want to do better. You are the most important person in the world to me; you are my life partner. I've decided I need to start showing you my appreciation." I sit stunned! Where did that come from? It's been six months, and my husband is a completely different person now. He takes out the trash, puts his laundry in the hamper, and cleans up after himself.

When there's a chore to do around the house, he's eager to get it done. He has even pulled back from spending so much time with his friends. We now have weekly dates and spend a lot more time talking to each other and enjoying the company.

To build the momentum of a shift in energy, this exercise needs to be repeated daily for about 10-20 minutes. The scenes and activities should change with each new journal entry. "If you're doing it right," I tell clients, "you will come to enjoy these little reveries so much that you'll go way beyond 20minutes a day." In particularly important relationships, I've spent up to 2 hours an evening writing multiple scripts—and the time that I spent paid off big league!

As you're writing these scripts, you are allowing yourself to expect something new. You are opening yourself to possibilities. You are also squelching your negative reactions by not writing about them. Little by little, proof of change will magically happen. With each new victory, you will move deeper into the shifted version of you and your relationship.

Just keep the scenes positive, and watch the shifts occur! Enjoy!

Reflection:

Did you smile during your reverie, or did you shake your head in absolute disbelief, unable to move your pen? Sometimes, we fear to dream because we think we'll be crushed if it doesn't come true.

If you refuse to dream, you get one guarantee: NOTHING different will happen. I guarantee you that if you spend time each day doing this exercise, you WILL see positive change. As you start seeing changes in your relationships, DO NOT question changes with the other person. Show your appreciation for the changes. TRUST that YOU are creating your relationship differently and act as though this is the way things are supposed to be. I know, it will seem amazing to you, but remember, the other person is not aware of the work you are doing.

Exercise XI. Rewind

Whew! You just lived through a dramatic argument with your best friend. You feel shaken, confused, and regretful. As the adrenalin rush subsides, feelings of remorse wash over you. Take a moment to write down your feelings. Examine them: do they recreate an all too familiar pattern? As you review the scene in your mind, go all the way back to the beginning of the day. Were you already in a foul mood? Had you been rehearsing your lines before you met up with your friend?

Next, rewrite the day in the way you wish it would've happened. Put emphasis on the calm, positive attitude you carry into the interaction. See a completely positive unfolding of events. See the two of you, peaceful and understanding of each other. Don't be surprised if you get an unexpected reconciliation shortly after completing this exercise. Do not be expectant of the other person to change; be receptive to whatever comes.

Additionally, you can apply this exercise to upcoming events that always seem to provoke conflict.

Reflection:

Has your vibration shifted around this argument? Do you feel calm and forgiving? This frequency will draw a new outcome between you.

Exercise XII. Silent Communication

As you lie in your bed at night, recall a troubled relationship. See yourself standing in front of the person. Focus on your heart energy. See your chest begin to glow in deep emerald green outlined in pink. Look deep in this person's eyes and acknowledge them as your teacher and mirror. Understand you've created this interaction to teach you something about yourself. Speak positive words to the person standing before you. Speak your desire for mutual harmony, compassion, and understanding. Repeat this exercise nightly until you see a shift in the relationship. The shift will begin in you, as a new feeling and new perspective of this person. If this person is to remain in your life beyond the lesson they brought, the shift in you will extend to them.

In the days that follow Exercises XI and XII, pay attention to the thoughts that pop into your head about the person from your exercises. What are they saying? Does it feel like you are having a conversation? You may be receiving telepathic messages from them. If the thoughts seem negative, change your thoughts to something else. If the negativity does not shift out, you may discontinue the exercise and keep your distance from the person. The universe may be indicating that your time together is finished, for now at least. If the thoughts are positive, you may feel inspired to reach out to the person.

In all relationships, give up any attempts at changing the other person. Just work on yourself and watch the corresponding relationship changes take place.

Chapter Five
Soul Mating

I'd like to give you a Christmas gift ☆
A pair of glasses with multiple lenses
☆ *To help the eyes see long ago*
Then you would know ☆
The reason for the music. ☆
☆
Venus Trines at Midnight, Linda Goodman ☆

Soul Mates: Who Are They?

People use the term soul mate flippantly, usually implying someone with whom they are deeply in love and who has proven to be ever-available, ever-understanding, and a "perfect" partner. Oh, boy, Hollywood has done a number on their heads! As you will come to understand, these are myths.

More accurately, soul mates are people that carry a similar energy essence that is recognizable by you. The similar energy essence is a marker of soul family membership. We all belong to soul families that have nothing to do with our earth families. In fact, soul mates seldom incarnate within the same genetic family. They often meet as strangers who share an irresistible pull to each other. It's a soul language they speak one to the other. No words are necessary. The vibrational pull speaks loud and clear.

Soul families consist of multiple souls that carry similar soul group lessons. It's like everyone is working on the same lesson, but from different angles. Within a soul family group, the individual members also exist within multiple versions of themselves, each carrying a similar vibrational essence. People often speak of

94

seeking a single soul mate; however, we have multiple soul mates available to us. Thus, when a relationship doesn't work out with one soul mate, no worries; we can move on to attract a better-fitted soul mate.

Soul families often incarnate in similar timelines. Vibrational matching then draws the individuals together. These relationships can carry intense feelings of love, hate, fear or all emotions combined! Although soul mate relationships change roles from lifetime to lifetime, we will be focusing on soul mate lovers here.

The successful mating of souls is very different than the mating of egos. It involves a different kind of love, a love that is enduring and unconditional. If you are seeking a peaceful, uneventful relationship that doesn't push you out of your comfort range, a soul mate relationship may not be what you truly seek. You would be better off partnering up with the first person that your personality finds compatible. These are your choices.

Soul mates truly test your tenacity and endurance for unconditional love. By unconditional love, I mean the ability to stay in a higher, vibrational space without the other person necessarily making you happy. It does not mean a willingness to take abuse, however. Soul mate relationships help expand your willingness and capacity to learn more about yourself than ever before. Soul mates unearth your deepest wounds and then put you in a hall of mirrors to reflect those wounds. You are finally forced to own up and shift out. Unfortunately, all this growth does not necessarily guarantee a lasting committed relationship. Oftentimes, soul mates do not enter long-term committed relationships. Soul mates come into your life to remind you of your soul intentions and often disappear once you are firmly on your path.

Typically, soul mate relationships do not sit still; they are in a continual cycle of growth and expansion. Soul mate interactions can be very brief, super-charged time capsules. They may roar into our lives and quickly disappear. Then later down the road, they may be rekindled. Breaks from soul mates can last decades, if not lifetimes.

Regardless of their last physical interaction, soul mates are never far energetically, not even in death. They can be accessed for guidance and assurance during separations, whether the soul mate is living or deceased. Later, we will explore ways to connect with soul mates when physical interaction isn't possible.

Soul mates will not bend to suit your needs. They require you to grow beyond your former ideas of self and love. If you are strong enough to go the mile, you will learn more about yourself, about your relationships, and about life. Be forewarned, though, the soul mate path is not for the lazy or mild. Acceptance of a soul mate relationship puts you firmly on the hero's journey: it will teach you a lion's courage, an ant's persistence, and a yogi's patience—all while you are discovering your authentic self.

Twin Flames

Twin Flames are the most romanticized of all! Theories go something like: we are each half a soul waiting for a reunion with our other half, known as the twin flame. The theory follows that enlightened wholeness will only occur after these two halves have reunited. Thus, dreamy lovers everywhere seek this phantom completion to accept they are finally with their true "One" and indeed whole. Who could blame them for dreaming? We drown in over-the-top romantic fairytales like "Beauty and the Beast," and movies like "The Notebook," that lure us into believing. These myths have shaped our society's idea of happy, ideal relationship.

At the beginning of my relationship adventures, I too, believed this mythology. However, it didn't add up. How could we be only half of ourselves? What a rip off for those who never meet a twin flame! And even worse, what happens when we meet a twin flame, and there is zero compatibility? I realized through researching psychology, mythology, and spirituality that all external people and events represent something deep within the person observing them. Sounds like quantum physics, doesn't it? Additionally, I found that the term "twin flame" is a recent introduction in literature.

From a spiritual perspective, romantic relationships are a means to an end, they are not the main event. They don't exist to "complete" you. Relationships occur to teach the person a deeper understanding of Self. You see, we each have an opposite gender polarity within ourselves. Famous Swiss Psychiatrist, Carl Jung used the term *anima* to describe "the inner figure of a woman held by a man," and *animus* to describe "the figure of a man at work in a woman's psyche." A woman's polarity would be her animus; a man's polarity would be his anima. Innately, we are all reaching for completion by merging with this polar self. This was the original meaning of marriage. Union then comes from a blending of two halves within the same person. After witnessing projections of the anima/animus as "The One," Jungian analyst, James Hollis, coined the term "Magical Other" "that there is one person out there who... will know what we want and meet those deepest needs; a good parent who will protect us from suffering and spare us the challenging journey of individuation." Doesn't that sound a lot like a twin flame? The twin flame phenomenon is merely an externalized metaphor that was meant to lead us back home to Self. Perhaps, the twin flame, then, is not someone out there, but really somebody *in here*.

Have you ever had a dream of an unbelievably elusive beautiful or heroic lover? The dream's emotional tone may have felt incredibly intense and overwhelming. You awoke strongly desiring the phantom lover. These special dreams prompt a reunion with your inner polar self. They are reminders of your soul's path toward maturation. The same thing happens when you interact with a soul mate who seems so very similar to you; you may want to call them a twin flame, but what they really are is a projection of the inner you. They stimulate you to remember the wholeness of who you really are, and just like the dream lover, they, too, often feel more dream-like than real.

The hopeless romantics, however, will forever seek an external, physical twin flame lover. Once, an author came to me convinced he had met his twin flame. He was writing a book about twin flame reunions and was convinced that he must make tantric love to this girl to cement their "soul-fated" union. Unfortunately, she wanted nothing to do with him. He mercilessly stalked her, trying to convince her that theirs was a divinely-fated relationship. It didn't end well.

It is said that when twin flames cannot bring together union, one is invariably blamed as "less evolved" and not quite ready for enlightenment in this lifetime. They must wait for another spin on the carousel. Perhaps, the next lifetime, they will be ready. In a roundabout way, I guess you could say this is correct, but it isn't about two humans. It's about the individual's willingness to merge with his inner self in wholeness. However, most folks are too busy projecting their inner self onto mere mortals! Most of the time, these twin flame, star-crossed lovers never do sustain a long-term relationship. Something or someone always comes between them. Perhaps, it's the universe offering the mortal a free pass from carrying the heavy burden of god or goddess traits.

I'll conclude by saying: the twin flame mythology is a metaphor for the true, divine lover that slumbers within, waiting for that special kiss of remembrance.

Evolved Relationships and the Purpose of Soul Mating

We hear reports that people are marrying late, if they marry at all. Watch pop culture, listen to pop, country and rap music, the messages all ring same: disillusionment in relationships, particularly in marriage. People realize that marriage hasn't worked out too well in the past. Even with technology lending a hand in dating, sex, and physical alterations, people are still a wee bit jaded! They've realized that, although they have multiple choices, human beings are still, at their core, the same. They love; they fight; they break up.

No longer can we be forced to remain in unhappy relationships by God, a binding legal contract, or expensive divorce settlements. People enter (and remain), in marriage because they see value in it. They believe the relationship will help them grow and evolve. The ideal relationship is an agreement between two healthy, autonomous individuals who are both seeking their highest potential. Unlike the past, people realize that relationships cannot make them whole. That approach has been proven to create the least likely successful unions. Conscious people now desire a union between two whole people who take full responsibility for their mutual happiness. Yes, they desire a union of souls, not of egos. They want the soul mate union as it was really meant to be, as a growth experience intended to evolve the soul. In all fairness however, not everyone is concerned with finding their soul mate. Many people are seeking companionship, not growth through relationship, and that is fine.

For all those who deeply desire a soul-mating, my intention is to help you achieve a joyful, ever-expansive relationship. To attract the highest form of a soul mate, you will want to shift to a personality that predominantly radiates optimism, joy, positive expectation, and hopefulness. People who enter a relationship from a personally full, abundant space, understand how to be responsible for their own feelings without placing another in the role of fulfilling them. In this way, they love unconditionally. Furthermore, when unwanted appears, as it always will, the joy-filled person will understand how to put their focus on what is wanted and shift themselves. In so doing, these relationships will continue to expand and grow to a better and better place, with much less chance of separations based on incompatibility. By first learning to place your focus on shifting yourself, you will already own the secret to resolving most grievances.

It's All in Your Intentions

If you are very specific in your desire for soul mating, you will overlook those who don't match your soul essence. During my 6-year single, dating spree, I knew I wasn't interested in any more non-soul mate partnerships. I wanted a depth of experience that I could not feel with other kinds of partners. As I met many soul mates, I instantly recognized my soul family essence. Thus, I engaged multiple soul mates simultaneously, until I met my husband, Matt. I spent brief periods with non-soul mates, who helped "lighten the mood," but my greatest feelings and challenges came through the soul mate exchanges.

Since you have many soul mates in any given lifetime, your current personality will attract you to a soul mate who matches your current vibrational range. You may not have spent much time, beforehand, preparing for a soul mate relationship; regardless, you will find many chances to clarify your needs and clarify what you need to shift, while moving through various experiences. During these exchanges, you may experience multiple soul mates as well as non-soul mates. It all depends on your intention. For example, if your vibrational set point is currently one of despair, you may attract a homeless soul mate, or a soul mate suffering from drug addiction. You may say at this stage, "Who cares? I'll just fix him up when I find him! If I get my soul mate, I'll be happy!" Not true. The vibration at which a soul mating begins will be more extreme than the vibration of other relationship types. Meaning? It will push you to the edge without letting up. From the beginning, shifting work will be much more difficult because you will be faced with: intensified emotions, your soul mate's obstacles, and your own unresolved wounds. Ideally, it will be best to do your shifting work to be the version, who is already living your ideal soul mate relationship, before committing. Otherwise, extreme storms could be coming.

As you move through different interactions, your vibration can be moved in any direction, from positive (more fulfilling), to negative (nightmares), and all shades between. If you continue along a specific vibrational wavelength, you will continue to attract people who match that pattern. However, once you shift vibrations, the soul mates you attract will begin to match the new set point. It is also entirely possible that soul mates, who were previously encountered, will begin matching the new vibration and return for a relationship. So, whether you experience multiple soul mate experiences or choose being alone until your ideal soul mate comes along, the choice is always yours…with neither choice being right nor wrong. Each choice carries its own benefits and challenges.

If you decide to jump right into the soul mate dating pool, you will gain many experiences that will help you expand your original desire. In other words, your current idea of soul mate will be very different than your later, fully developed idea of a soul mate. Sure, you will experience loss as most of these interactions are not enduring, but you will come to understand that each loss is preparing you for the next level of soul mating. Furthermore, there's no such thing as "running out" of soul mates. In previous myths, we were taught to believe if we couldn't be with our one true soul mate or twin flame, we were forever doomed with heartache. Many stories, like the Arthurian Tales of unrequited love between Lancelot and Guinevere, echoed this sentiment. With our new understanding of multiple timelines, multiple particles, and multiple soul mates, we release the fear of unrequited and lost love once and for all!

Thus, "the One" turns out to be the one you are currently matching. So, enjoy multiple soul mates or wait for just one, but know this: each interaction helps you "grow" your ultimate, ideal relationship. You can build better and better relationships with multiple partners because you are doing the shifting work while relating, or you can do the shifting work alone until you match up with your ideal. The advantage of multiple relationships is that they offer evaluations of where you need to continue shifting.

Throughout your lifetime, your higher self has been listening in, tracking all your despairs and desires. As each new desire is born, your higher self automatically creates your desires, as particle realities, and holds the space for you to match them. Where do these manifestations exist? Well, you already know where—they exist in the field. Through the exercises in this book, you will understand how to continuously shift to better and improved personalities, each living different versions of your desires. You will embrace the goodies your higher self has been holding for you.

With all of this said, do you understand there are no wrong relationship choices? Do you understand that the ending of a relationship is not a failure? Your choices are yours alone. Each choice presents you with a new path, full of new understanding and opportunity for growth. No one can make your choices for you. And at any given time, you may change your choices. A choice, once made, does not automatically lock you into a path forevermore. Remember that.

And now, it's time to learn how to recognize a person as your soul mate.

Soul Mate Clues, (not a dozen roses)

Last night I had a dream.
You came into my room,
You took me into your arms.
Whispering and kissing me,
And telling me to still believe.

When I awoke I cried again for you were gone.
Oh, can you hear me?

"It Can't Rain All the Time," Jane Siberry
The Crow: original motion picture soundtrack

Soul mate interactions are typically marked by a certain intense energy between both people. The intensity stems from recognition of the soul family essence and is felt as a subconscious knowing. If the initial response is positive, the interaction will feel like a homecoming. Feelings of knowingness, appreciation, attraction or love may wash over the individuals. If the initial response is negative, feelings of instant dislike, competition, distrust and even hatred, may cloud the present moment. Remember my introductory story about Josh? Whatever that initial meeting holds, it seldom feels neutral as does non-soul mate interactions. The feelings are often compulsive, as though the soul mates know there is something important to accomplish. So, we are drawn to soul mates like moths to flames, and often, we get burned.

I believe that most people we meet are not soul mates. Soul mates may fall into a variety of roles: friend, lover, or enemy, but one thing is for sure, all soul mates come as teachers. During pre-incarnation, soul mates make agreements to enter each other's lives as an act of loving service. To be romantic or committed lovers is not the soul mate's highest goal. As soul mates come from our own soul group, they innately understand the intentions of our soul. Soul mates will mirror our deepest lifetime wounds, and the healing of these wounds brings us our greatest lifetime soul achievement. Do you think these lessons are filled with roses and chocolates? Think again.

Simply put: soul mates aren't what most people think they are. Due to the multitude of lifetimes we live, we incarnate with new soul lessons each lifetime. In one lifetime, we may experience lessons in compassion; in another lifetime, we may experience the perspective of sacrifice and service, and still another lifetime, we may live with lessons in abandonment. The roles are endless and ever-changing because we want to experience all human perspectives. Thus, our soul mate relationships highlight the lessons our soul wants to learn in the particle reality we are living.

We partner with soul mates in the most unique, unexplainable circumstances. Soul mates are often unusually matched and labeled taboo by societal standards such as by marked age differences (7++ years), different races, same sex genders, different religions, extreme physical/emotional/mental imbalances.

Obviously, not every couple who claim the above categories are soul mates. However, soul mate relationships almost always re-define popular concepts of love & relationship. Soul mating opens complex Pandora's Boxes with lots to teach the soul mates, their biological families, and society. Soul mates' subtle messages go beyond illusions and sink right down to Truth.

The most frequent timing of soul mate matching occurs around life crises like terminal illness, death, and divorce. Regarding marriage crises, everything seems stable on the home front, when suddenly a spouse meets a soul mate. The intensity of the soul mate energy compels the spouse to make abrupt, long needed changes. The marriage has been on life support for many years, and it took this stick of dynamite to blast the partners beyond their ruts. The promise of new love is a very strong motivating factor to move people in a new direction. Unfortunately, once the marriage is officially over, the soul mates often go their separate ways. The bewildered divorcee calls me shattered. They don't remember their soul mate agreement was for soul growth, not necessarily romance.

Pay attention to the timing of your soul mate's appearance. The events surrounding the initial interactions will often reveal the soul mate's true purpose in your life. Following or during pivotal life events, the soul mate's message is one of support, comfort, and confirmation toward major life changes. Try not to attach any single outcome to your soul mate's appearance. Be curious and enjoy the energy without expectations. I know, easier said than done.

In my astrology work, I examine client compatibility charts, looking for the obvious soul mate signatures, as clients are seeking confirmation for their strange pull to specific people. Soul mate astrology reveals interplanetary aspects that define feelings, obstacles, soul growth lessons, and longevity of the connection. Without getting too complex here, I will say that personal planets such as the Sun, Moon, Mercury, Venus & Mars are always tied to the higher learning planets of Saturn, Uranus, Neptune & Pluto. The interplanetary connections between charts are usually tense aspects reflective of the serious work being done in the relationship. Ironically, the more difficult the lessons, the more compelling is the relationship, ensuring that the soul mates stick together until the lessons are completed.

During my interactions with Josh, he felt very much like what people describe as "twin flames." As I admired him in human form, I recognized him as the perfect reflection of my inner self. Studying our astrology charts, I saw every single soul mate, lover, & commitment planetary marker. It was a pretty perfect astrological union. However, our charts showed us to never consummate our relationship beyond a spiritual love. Thus, when people come to me assured theirs is "the love of all loves," I caution them not to assume anything about the interaction, knowing time will spin the tale.

Psychic Perceptions between Soul Mates

And her eyes immediately met those
of a large, blue caterpillar
that was sitting on the top with its arms folded, quietly
smoking a long hookah...
The caterpillar and Alice
looked at each other for some time in silence.

Alice's Adventures in Wonderland, Lewis Carroll

Before I teach you these powerful, magical tools, I want to make it very clear that I am not an advocate of attempts to manipulate or control another human being. Period! While I do not believe we can "make" people do something against their will, I do acknowledge our power to influence others. Meaning, the psychically inexperienced person may be overwhelmed and impacted by a more powerful, manipulative, or focused energy— for a time. Fortunately, these situations are usually of short duration, unless the person has been severely abused and is lacking personal boundaries.

Sending out positive, goodwill towards healthy individuals is more readily accepted into their experience than negative, manipulative agendas. However, a person of long standing abuse has weaker boundaries and holes in their aura. They will often adopt another's energy without realizing what they are doing. Please realize that energy flows both ways. If you hold negative intentions toward another, be rest assured, that energy will return to you. Also, when you focus on a person, you will start to match their vibration. If this isn't a vibration conducive to your well-being, you may decide to limit your focus and shift focus toward a higher vibration alternate version of the person, which also implies a higher vibration version of you.

With all of that said, I will add that you will sense when your psychic work is an intrusion. What do I mean? During your exercises, you will sense the other person becoming agitated, angry, or avoidant. At that point, it is your responsibility to pull back; otherwise, the consequences can ultimately lead to estrangement from your partner. No one likes to feel that someone is trying to force them beyond their will.

Through this experience of soul mating, you will find your love spanning time and space. Soul mate love is really quantum love. In most attractions between people, lust drives the chemistry. Once that lust has been satiated, there's nothing left between the individuals. Also, if someone cannot bear distance from a lover, they call me panicked when they go a few weeks without interaction (as though their love will run dry if not recharged by interaction). The incessant need for constant stimulation and reassurance lets me know we aren't talking about soul mate love. In soul mate love, you will come to realize how love endures beyond a simple, "out of sight, out of mind" fleeting feeling. No matter how many months or years you two are separated, the feelings come alive when you are reunited. You will also realize that you are not quick to replace the person with another "easier" relationship.

Although I was born an empath and exhibited psychic skills my entire life, I did not consciously direct or understand many of my psychic skills until I began experiencing multiple soul mate relationships. We are all born with these psychic gifts; however, most of us do not have the desire or motivation to hone these skills—until love is involved. Your psychic skills are very much like any other talent—they grow with repeated practice.

I once had a Scorpio client who kept calling about her Aries soul mate. In true soul mate fashion, he came into her life at the end of her crumbling marriage. She wanted guarantees of relationship if she divorced her husband. The Aries wasn't offering it. I explained the soul growth behind this relationship and its timing. I also taught her the psychic perception exercises. She would call and say, "I know this sounds crazy, but I felt him thinking about me sexually last night." No, not crazy; she was probably tuned into one of his fantasy sessions. The next week, she would say, "I feel like he really worries about my marriage." True again. Eventually, she learned to trust her perceptions and stopped calling.

Your inborn psychic skills are just another language that you can learn to use in a consistent, effective, practical way. These skills are a direct link to the vibrational world of energy and your higher self. Thus, by learning to use these skills daily, you are enhancing your experience as a human and as a lover. There will be times when direct, open communication with your partner is not possible, and you will need to fall back on these developed skills.

As we focus energy, particles begin their forward push to manifestation. However, before our human senses realize physical manifestation, a ghost form exists in the astral realm. These ghost forms can be interpreted through visions, feelings, words, smells, and touch. Clairvoyance, clairsentience, clairolfaction, psychometry, clairaudience, and telepathy are a few of the psychic skills we will be discussing.

Psychic skills are found in the playground of quantum physics. They do not follow quantifiable, measurable methods. Psychic skills can dip you into parallel realities, and drop kick you into past/present/future time lines simultaneously. People scoff at psychic skills just because they can't be "proven." I get at least one message a week starting with: "You're going to think I'm crazy, but I had the weirdest thing happen."

People using psychic skills often rely on certain skills to the exclusion of others. While I may get a feeling about someone, another person may see a symbolic vision of the person. Thus, you will want to try your hand at each of the following skills to determine which one is the right "fit" for your unique style.

Psychic Skills

To the unenlightened man, this will seem to be all fantasy, yet all progress comes from those who do not take the accepted view, nor accept the world as it is.

The Power of Awareness, Neville Goddard

While most people do not consciously recognize or accept their true feelings or thoughts, they will not welcome your psychic perceptions about them either, even when they ask you. There's something strangely spooky about another person knowing your private self, especially when you're not even acknowledging this self. Therefore, mostly, you will not receive concrete, factual confirmation of your psychic skills, and it will be at these times that you will need to trust yourself. Do not mistake me; these are not "free for all" mind reading techniques. You will not be able to scan your lover's mind and know everything they are thinking. That would be invasive. What you will learn how to do is skip through the games and denials to understand the truth about what is happening between you. You will also bypass the middleman, psychic, to get your own answers.

The art of "seeing" visions, such as the ones you received from the "Field of Dreams" exercise, is called **clairvoyance.** Psychic skills do not depend on the five physical senses; thus, you cannot "see" with your physical eyes. The seeing is an internal perception through the pineal gland, third eye lens. To clairvoyantly "see" is to receive an impression that your mind then processes into a visual picture. So, you do not see with your external eyes; you see with your inner eye.

During waking moments, you may receive clairvoyant visions of your mate. These visions are not limited to present lives. They can spontaneously occur in any timeline involving past or future lives or alternate timelines and probabilities. I received a vision of Matt and I in 18th century France. We were both attending a ball, and I was wearing an exquisitely opulent dress. We were secret lovers who stole away from the ball for a passionate rendezvous in one of the palace halls.

Clairsentience is the talent of "feeling" a person's energy nearby. I've been lying in bed and felt the presence of a soul mate. I felt his rough beard, silky hair, and strong muscular arms. These feelings can be so strong that you will almost believe your soul mate is there with you—and a part of them is.

On many occasions, I'd be in public places and catch a soul mate's cologne wafting on the wind. **Clairolfaction** is the psychic gift of smelling energy. Just like the other psychic senses, it may not necessarily be an actual smell you receive with your nose. The energy may be interpreted as a tangible fragrance or odor. Deceased people will often signal their presence by their signature scent. Once, while doing a reading, a lady asked how she would know real contact from her deceased sister. Matter-of-factly, I chimed, "It will be like sitting on the couch, and you catch the smell of roses, with roses being her favorite flower." My client shot back, "THAT would be her!!!! She wore rose perfume!"

If your desire for physical contact is strong enough, and you are receptive, you can tune into your soul mate's energy. For me, I have experienced clairsentience and clairolfaction mostly through spontaneous incidences that were beyond my focused attention. Lost in thought, I'd be in a public place and suddenly feel or smell him. My clairsentient and clairolfaction episodes always signaled that periods of long separations were about to end. Remember, the vibration exists before the manifestation, so when you tune in psychically to pre-manifested energy, the manifestation is not far behind.

I've also been surprised by feeling my soul mate's presence through a nearby stranger carrying similar energy essence. One night, I was in a restaurant waiting line, and I suddenly felt "him" standing behind me. I swirled around to find a stranger standing there. After a few of these events, I began to realize that different individuals carry same soul essences. We will discuss this phenomenon in more detail in Chapter 6.

Additionally, touching a person's personal items for psychic impressions, **psychometry**, can also help you connect with their energy. We smile at teenage girls who wear their boyfriend's jackets, as we think they're overly sentimental. However, the act of touching the boyfriend's personal item is an effective way of connecting with his energy. During a very scary episode in Matt's life, we were physically separated. I clung to his shirt and belt to send him love and strength.

Clairaudience enables us to hear unspoken words. With this skill, energy is interpreted through inner hearing. You may be far away from your partner and hear them speaking to you. The first time this happened to me, I was sitting alone on my couch late one night. I was quietly reading without any external sound in the house. Suddenly, I began hearing people talking, as if they were on the phone, and I was eavesdropping on their conversation. The second time I experienced clairaudience, I heard my lover call my name, even though he was 1400 miles away. The sound was very clear and very strong, and I promptly looked up, as if to say, "What?"

Telepathy: A New Way of Communicating

The art of telepathy involves sending and receiving messages to each other without any spoken communication occurring. Throughout time, telepathy has always occurred just beneath the surface of consciousness. As a species, we are now on the brink of learning to consciously direct our telepathic messages. Just look at the evolution of our communication systems; our technology, with its texting, instant messaging, and camera talking, is preparing us for everyday telepathic communications. These processes are speeding up our ability to communicate without time or space restrictions. We are learning to communicate more quickly, directly, and honestly, until one day, we will discover that we no longer need "devices" to communicate over short or long distances.

How many times have you held a conversation with someone in your head? You probably didn't realize that you were truly sending and receiving thoughts. As you are reading this book, and say, you are thinking about your mate in South Africa, you are sending telepathic communications to her. Until now, you were largely unaware of these communications. You may have thought it a strange coincidence when she unexpectedly calls to say, "I was just thinking about you." Many of the exercises in this book involve telepathy, therefore, a person who continues interaction is most likely accepting of your intentions because they've already received several telepathic messages from you.

Telepathy is focusing energy toward a subject. It is not to be forced, although it happens all the time just beneath conscious awareness. As you think of another and engage one-sided conversations with them, these silent communications do find their way to your subject. Because telepathy is a continuous stream, we seldom recognize the messages as we are receiving them. It is also difficult to know where the communication began—with you or with your partner. Matt and I are so energetically intertwined that one of us will think a thought, and the other will verbally respond. Our soul mate Persian, Sir Gawain, enjoys our telepathic conversations. He's able to communicate his needs quite efficiently. All animals use telepathy, and lucky is the one who finds a human who can talk back!

It is easiest to detect telepathic messages when you spontaneously think of someone. I often begin thinking of regular clients before their phone call. Once, one of Mystical Empress's psychics went out of town for a funeral. She called to tell me that I would need to cancel a scheduled reading she had in 2 weeks. I opened my calendar and realized that I had not taken the client's phone number! Oh no! Within one hour, the client called and said she wished to move up her appointment. I told her, "You are much more psychic than you realize! Thank you for responding to my message!"

Consequently, when you think of someone in anger, they are picking up your messages of anger. With telepathy, it's impossible to hide anything. So, the next time you find yourself upset with your lover, guard your thoughts carefully. Do not send out any mental communications—unless they are pleasant. Otherwise, be prepared to receive their response either telepathically, verbally, or you may notice them avoiding you.

I often send telepathic messages to a person when I've changed my mind and do not want to do something we've agreed to do, like a meeting. I live spontaneously and flow with the different rhythms of the day. Thus, plans made in advance, may need to change. When I realize I need to do something else, or I'm just not in the mood to do the planned thing, I telepathically send a message to the other person and then allow them to contact me with *their changed plans*. The only way this will work is if I expect it to work. If I continue thinking about my new decision and justifying it, then I will either need to meet my obligation or call it off myself.

In the beginning of your psychic journey, your easiest way of distinguishing the difference between your own mental chatter and actual telepathic connection is by keeping your thoughts clear of the person until the actual connection is desired. In this way, you can pick up when they are sending energy to you. If your mind is already full of thoughts about a person, it is much more difficult to distinguish your thoughts from their thoughts.

When you can clear your mind of other people, you will sense their energy as it comes into your awareness. You may be lost in an activity and suddenly think of your mate. This is a telepathic thought form coming from them. Do not discount it.

You may choose telepathic communications before interaction with your soul mate, especially when the interaction may feel threatening to them. Telepathy is an effective tool in pre-paving upcoming meetings, resolving disagreements, and clarifying our feelings in a non-threatening way.

As you start sensing energy fields, you will want to learn to distinguish your energy field from your mate's energy. Energy fields are like thumbprints; they are uniquely your own. As you become more adept at sensing the energy field of your mate, you will not necessarily need as much open mind space to pick up on them. Once you learn to distinguish the energy as separate, then you can learn to decipher what the energy is telling you.

Telepathy can be used in many valuable ways. Used with children and pets, you can understand their unspoken needs. Business meetings and dates can be pre-paved for optimal outcomes. When a client is estranged from someone, I often advise them to start a gentle telepathic conversation to sooth feelings and check receptivity.

Astral Travel & Dreamtime

For interactions beyond the physical body, you can travel via your astral double. This shadow replication of you is not constrained by the 3D rules of space and time. Thus, your astral double can travel to foreign lands and universes in the blink of an eye. It knows no barriers. Astral travel usually happens during periods of sleep and deep meditation. You may recall your adventures as a "dream"; however, there will be a real intensity of presence that is not paralleled in dreams. A psychically sensitive person may even witness your visit.

Most of our interactions with the dead are through dreamtime travels. Dreamtime parts the veil of separation. During this time, our consciousness is much more open to psychic phenomenon. How do you know if you've had one of these visits? You will awaken feeling the strong presence of that person. The energy of a dream is much more spacy and symbolic. It's not as sharply focused.

While you are in a human body, you're connected to your higher self through a silver energy cord that connects your body to your higher self. This cord is not broken until the moment of your death. Thus, there is nothing to fear along the lines of being "lost between worlds" during astral travels. Prepare for your journey by choosing a positive state of mind, creating a protective golden barrier around your body, and then intending safety for your traveling consciousness and your resting body. In this way, you will only meet with happy travels.

Your desire for an astral meeting will attract the circumstances for a journey. As in all things, intensely felt desire creates the manifestation quickly, with one stipulation: you must not be focusing on anything that opposes the desire. Therefore, it is imperative to be open to the experience; otherwise, it will not happen. Sometimes people fear astral travel, and they short circuit the trip by snapping back into their bodies.

When seeking previously undisclosed information, ask your mate to share it with you in dreamtime. You may ask questions of your mate right before sleep time. Remember however, your subconscious deals in the vocabulary of symbols. You may receive direct, literal words, but mostly, you will receive answers steeped in symbols. If you repeatedly dream your mate is unwilling to engage, this is a sign of their resistance.

A story worth sharing involves one of my soul mates who visited me in dreams. After we broke up, he continued to express his longing for me in dreamtime. I even received dreams about our wedding, which I now suspect were alternate realities. I misinterpreted these dreams as him wanting to get back together. I approached him, and he vehemently denied his feelings. I respected his boundaries and moved on, even though psychically, I knew he was deeply in love with me. Looking back, I can only imagine his shock that I had knowledge of his true feelings. Even now, years later, I can still feel him thinking of what might have been between us.

Exercise XIII. Part 1: Soul Mate Sacred Space

Begin by imagining a pleasant, neutral, safe location in your mind. Choose scents, sounds, colors, & images that are peaceful and soothing. Add as many sensory details as necessary to make this scene real for you. It is crucial that this setting is free of any distractions or negativity. An example would be riding in a rowboat on a calm lake, or sitting in a lush, comforting forest. I once created a soul mate sacred space in an enchanted forest. A lush, four posted bed was at the center of the forest. The point is to choose a place of comfort & serenity. This will be your sacred soul mate space. Do not use it for any form of disagreements, upsets, or negativity. For an added dimension to the sacredness of this space, ask your favorite Archangel or Enlightened Master to fill the space with Divine love. State your prayer, "Archangel Gabriel, please fill this space with your enlightened energy, love, and healing. Thank you."

Form your mate's image before you. You will immediately get a clue here on your mate's willingness to cooperate. If their image is difficult to form or sustain, end the session because they are not open. If you can easily hold the image, and even better, if you can feel a strong presence with the image, congratulations! You've achieved connection!

If it feels appropriate, and your mate seems willing, hold your hand to their heart while they hold their hand to yours. This denotes heartfelt communication. Next, look in your soul mate's eyes and speak. By speaking to the eyes, you are bypassing the ego and connecting with the true essence of your mate. If they wish to speak, they will respond.

If they refuse interaction or the communication feels forced, end the session because they are unwilling to interact. We must respect boundaries, even on the psychic level. You may think the other person will not be aware of your unwanted psychic intrusions, but think again. They will feel a sense of unease or distrust around you and may even cut off interaction altogether. Also, when you force the interaction, information received is not the truth. It is merely your mind filling in the blanks and not a true two-way interaction.

Part 2: Astral Sex

I have repeatedly gone back and forth on writing this section. I almost deleted it because I did not want to offer a tool that unscrupulous people could use against other unsuspecting people. I do not appreciate manipulation of any sort, including energetic. The sex drive is one of the most powerful drives humans are given; therefore, it is difficult to predict what people will do with such profound wisdom. In the end, I decided to share the information, and I intend it be used in the highest light. As I've experienced sexual psychic invasion, I also felt it important to alert my readers of these possibilities. Remember: in all things psychic, respect boundaries. I know it seems like it's just "make believe," but as you do these exercises, you will come to know it is very real. Use your power respectfully, or be prepared for that power to be used against you.

During your private sessions, you or your mate may feel deep sexual stirrings that prompt you toward release. You may choose to create lovemaking scenes within your sacred space. Astral sex brings up very intense feelings. Sexual intertwining in this imaginal world can be the most intense and profound of your sexual encounters, simply because there is no resistance blocking the energy flow between you. In this realm of non-resistance, deep feelings are expressed, and intense physical longings flow. By engaging in astral sex with your soul mate, you may stimulate strong unconscious sexual desire toward you—from your mate and other outside sources.

I've encountered clients who have engaged in astral sex with dark entities, also known as incubus (male demon), and succubus (female demon). These interactions are to be avoided at all costs because they set up attachments and possessions that can be difficult to cancel. On two occasions, my male clients said that it was easier to engage these entities than to interact with real women. I am not encouraging this unhealthy pattern that takes you away from your human focus. In preparing for astral sex, I strongly advise that you intend interactions with healthy, living human beings because astral sex with dark entities and discarnate beings will open a nasty can of worms.

How do you know if it is ok to create a sacred space of astral lovemaking? It is the same as with all scene writing. If the images & words flow easily, your partner is a willing participant. If you have difficulty keeping the focus and/or experience resistance from your partner, stop immediately. If they are not in agreement with your desire, your pushing may result in a repulsion toward you. This is known as psychic invasion, and it is NOT okay.

This goes for the influence of random sexual thoughts coming toward you, also. I was awakened between 2-3am every night for a week with thoughts of intense sexual desire for one of my soul mates, although we had never been physically intimate. When I brought these promptings to his attention, he merely responded with a smug smile. I knew that he was also aware of energy molding techniques, and I knew he was engaging in astral sex with me.

Another example comes from a former bisexual female friend. There was never any discussion of any romantic or sexual relations between us. She was a very sexual person, and she'd entertain me for hours with her tales of sexual seduction. She always remarked how women and men couldn't restrain themselves around her. She made it sound like she was an irresistible sex magnet. After a time, I started noticing that our visits were always clouded by an extremely powerful sexual energy. Once, my ex-husband even asked if I had been sexual with her during a visit. As the years wore on, and I knew a meeting was coming, I noticed having all these unusual sexual thoughts about her. I'd think, "Why am I having these sexual stirrings? I'm not gay, and I am not sexually attracted to her. What is this about?" In those days, I wasn't as versed in psychic energies, so I just kind of shrugged it off. Eventually, I came to understand that she was trying to psychically seduce me. The sexual energy she was sending me was extremely powerful and focused, so I could see why so many people succumbed to her intentions. As she was a practicing witch, she knew how to direct energy. From this experience, I realized how undisciplined, unconscious people could easily slide into sexual liaisons and later regret them.

A word about astral affairs:

What you do on the astral level is very much "doing" a thing. You may rationalize that you are not having an affair with a married man because there are no physical interactions. However, vibration always precedes manifestation, meaning, you've already created the vibrational space through focused attention toward the desired result. It does exist. It is happening. Through repeated visioning, the physical manifestation has every possibility of occurring. Passion unhindered by resistance is an extremely powerful thought form, and this passionate expression propels manifestation swiftly. Do not be surprised (or offended), when your next in-person encounter with your fantasy lover is highly charged.

But Is This Ethical?

> *For unto whomsoever much is given, of him shall*
> *be much required: and to whom men have committed*
> *much, of him they will ask the more.*
>
> *Luke 12:48*

As in the bisexual girlfriend paragraph, it is highly unethical to try to force your sexual or relationship agenda on someone you already know is unwilling. I've received many calls from men and women asking for spells to break up marriages and force people to be with them. I flatly refuse to engage such destructiveness. I refuse because the intention is dishonorable and manipulative, and I know that something done with negative intent will come back to the offending party.

Let's explore: A single female has read this book and has now set her sights on her married co-worker. In addition to doing the exercises in this book, she finds a love spell guaranteed to bring her lover to her. She doesn't really get a sense of cooperation in her exercises, but she completes them faithfully anyway. She flirts with her co-worker, making it known that she's interested. He nervously smiles and shies away from interaction with her. One night, the man receives devastating news, and he's mentally weak. The female sees her opportunity, places herself strategically, and he gives in. They end up in a passionate sexual encounter. An hour later, he realizes he's just made the biggest mistake of his life! He never wanted to have an affair. He loves his wife. Afterward, he discreetly distances himself from his co-worker. In this scenario, there wasn't a matching particle of the two in a relationship. The woman's previous manifesting efforts have accumulated in a vortex of attraction; thus, she may go on to attract someone who is available and willing to relate. However, if her pattern is to seek non-available partners, like married men, she will repeat a similar seduction scenario all over again. Due to her manipulative intentions, she may find herself embroiled in a pretty nasty power struggle with her next lover.

When a person is not willing to take your relationship to the next step, there is no obvious flow to the psychic interactions, and the energy feels forced. Under these circumstances, it is best to respect boundaries and move on. If you continue pushing interaction, you will be setting up a nasty energetic pattern. Consequently, you will then meet this pattern in other interactions.

The field contains many, many different versions of reality. By choosing a particle reality that fits your desires, you are not taking away the free will of another. This is a universe of abundance, and there is no competition over limited opportunities or resources.

Each person is equally creating their own reality by the particles they choose. Consciously, you can never be aware of their personal particle realities. Even when a person blames you for something not to their liking, you are still creating the blame in your reality. For their part, the other person has every opportunity to create their desire (opposite from yours) in their own particle reality. Just as you cannot create their reality, they cannot create yours. If a person does not have a matching version of your desire, they will not engage you.

In the relationship exercises, you may choose one of 2 scenarios: you may insert a specific person in your work, or you may leave it open, without scripting a specific person. Clients ask me: "So how do I know this person is the one for my exercises?" I say, "Ask for a vision of the two of you together. If you cannot get one after repeated attempts, you will be better off leaving the space open." I did it both ways. I could tell from my journaling work that the other soul mates were not in alignment with my relationship desire. Thus, I mostly left my scripting open until I met Matt.

Unwanted Psychic Intrusions

In all psychic areas, it is important to remember: 1) that your mate may not be consciously aware of the information you receive 2) that the information can be symbolic and not literal 3) that it is your responsibility to respect boundaries and not force any interactions. Some people do not care about boundaries; they only care about their own agenda.

In the beginning of my psychic path, I parted ways from a friend who told me that she knew how to "make people do what she wanted them to do." Upon our separation, I began feeling a very intense "pulling at me" from her. I knew it was her because she filled my mind with unwanted telepathic communications. The energy was overwhelming, and I could see how an unwary person could succumb to it. This type of energetic pull stems from a dysfunctional, manipulative mentality and is surprisingly common in unbreakable, unhealthy partnerships that cannot seem to separate. As these power struggle methods are not conducive to love, harmony or healthy relating, I strongly advise against them. Any way you look at them, power struggles are not about love.

Our first impressions of a person are 99.9% accurate. In our initial meetings with someone, before we know their personality or story, we are psychically reading them by their aura's vibration. We may not be able to verbalize where the information is coming from, but it doesn't matter. The aura does not lie.

Trust & acknowledge the impressions that you receive. Then proceed with caution. Every soul mate interaction, whether brief or long-term, is valuable to your evolving consciousness. I must admit too, regardless of the initial impression, you will probably still desire interaction. The pull is very strong.

When we are completely honest with ourselves, we often intuit from the first few meetings how the interactions will evolve. We may feel a stabbing pain of unrequited love. We may sense that we are going to be hurt by this interaction. We may know that a person cannot be trusted. In my own experiences, I encountered soul mate men who had experienced severe abuse and were incapable of opening to soul mate depth love. They were irresistibly drawn to the energy, often despite themselves. In the end, they were completely unable to cultivate the level of relationship I was intending. Although the situations persisted, sometimes for years,

I always knew that things were not going to progress to the relationship that I was seeking. When I attempted to do visualizations, I felt their receptivity, but my mind would only create short term interactions. Later, I learned this meant we did not exist in other particle realities together. There were no matching versions to sustain a relationship.

Exercise XIV. Cutting Psychic Chords

This exercise should be done periodically with everyone you know, to regain a sense of your own energy. The more psychically sensitive you are, the more you will tend to lose yourself in relationships. After a time, you forget who you are and what you need. In addition, this exercise should be completed at the end of any relationship.

To conclude a relationship or interaction, you must divert thoughts about the person out of your conscious awareness. Every time you think of someone, you recharge the psychic cord between you. Also, do not have any physical interaction with them for you are reactivating the psychic cord. Sexual activity really ties you into a person psychically.

At the end of a relationship: Go into meditation and see the person standing before you. Hold your hand over your heart and say, "Thank you for being my teacher. I have learned your lessons well, and I am now releasing you from my experience. Go in peace." Then ask Archangel Michael to use his sword to cut all psychic chords between you. See him cutting connecting spaghetti strings between you and the person you are releasing. See the chords falling off the front and back of your body. Afterward, see a golden ball of light surrounding you.

For maintenance: Go into meditation and call on Archangel Michael to clear all psychic chords from your body. If you have some particularly intense attachments with certain people, be sure to see the chords attached to them being cleared in the visualization. This exercise does not terminate relationships; it just puts you back in your energetic space and puts the other people back in their space. Afterward, see a golden ball of light surrounding you.

As soon as you start thinking about a person or interacting with them, you resume psychic chords. Please note: if you are wanting to end a relationship, and you continue to sleep next to a person and/or continue sexual relations with them, these psychic cords will remain intact and make it harder for you to break away.

Chapter Six
Evolving Relationships

Life is a process of becoming, a combination of states we have to go through. Where people fail is that they wish to elect a state and remain in it. This is a kind of death.

Anais Nin

The Wheel Never Stops Spinning

As we move through life, our experiences birth new desires. These new desires demand a corresponding personality to match them. What doesn't change, hardens into resistance. Life is a very dynamic process; however, most people do not understand the powerful energy of change. If we are not continuously growing & shifting into new identities & realities, we meet with frustration. Left unchanged, frustration eventually dips into anger, depression & hopelessness. These lower vibrational emotions breed bodily decline and illness.

By blaming our partners, our children, and our parents for our unhappiness, we miss the creative ability to expand our lives into something more fulfilling. The bottom line is: if you want your relationships to stay harmonious and fulfilling, you must continue to evolve them. In our ever-increasing resistance to life, we naturally project our unease and unhappiness onto our key relationships, especially our love relationships. Most people stop focusing on their love relationship after they have a) achieved marriage b) had kids c) established a career path. Marriage is not an end goal, it is an ever-evolving state of togetherness. To continue any kind of healthy functioning relationship, we must be willing to evolve our interactions.

Life Transitions

Life offers us signposts to evaluate our progress and to stimulate us toward growth. So many of us want the status quo never to change; however, without change, we stagnate and decline. We came into these bodies for continual growth, and when our human minds refuse growth, life has a way of pushing us out of our ruts!

We most often notice life's milestones in our varying ages and life events like our 20's, 30's, 40's or leaving home, marriage, childbirth, divorce, mid-life crisis, empty nest, and retirement. As these milestones are reached, pressure builds for us to examine our lives. We gauge our successes and our failures and may see ourselves as falling short of where we expected to be in our lives.

Through the lens of astrology, we can see specific cycles that occur at certain ages and how long they will last. The more psychically sensitive a person is, the earlier they will feel upcoming cycles, often up to a year in advance. While I do not recommend being chained to any external timing device, knowledge of these broad cycles will help you adjust to the changes as they occur. Interestingly, these planetary cycles also correspond to many socially accepted life changes.

Saturn Return

Clients in their late 20's are often frantic considering things such as marriage, divorce, childbirth, career changes, and relocation. I know they are in their Saturn return, which occurs between ages 28 to 30. I soothe them by explaining all the confusion they are feeling is quite natural. Saturn is the planet of crystallization and turning points. Saturn locks in Earth's energies as we progress throughout our lifetime. During the first Saturn return, young adults are learning the consequences of their decisions. I encourage them to choose wisely because these choices will mark much of their adult lives. Relationships that will not support their path fall away. Relationships of a karmic nature, including soul mates, are often discovered.

7 Year Saturn Cycles

Ever heard of the 7-year itch? Saturn marks significant turning points every seven years. During these 7-year cycles, Saturn pushes us toward a restructuring and revaluation of our lives. Crisis may be involved to ensure changes are made. I've found that many adults, who are on the brink of necessary internal changes, project these changes externally onto their love relationships. While many times these relationships do need changing, they are still only symbols reflecting deeper issues.

Uranus Opposition

Another major cycle is the Uranus opposition, which happens between ages 39 to 41. This is a big one because it offers the most obvious quantum shifts. Uranus is the planet of sudden changes, rebellion, eccentricity and the absolute demand to live life on your own terms. When talking to clients in their Uranus opposition, I say, "It's like your soul is stepping in and saying, "Ok, you've lived your life according to society's expectations, now it's time to live the authentic you! It's time to throw off the shackles and dare to walk through a new door." I see people quitting their jobs, leaving their marriages, and changing their social circle. All the while their friends predictably say, "It's just a mid-life crisis." Yes, it is a crisis, but it's much more than that. It's time that marks the rest of your life's progression. Based on choices made here, you will go out in a blaze of glory or slowly wither on the vine. This cycle is one of the most obvious attempts for soul growth.

If you find yourself in this cycle, embrace Uranus' propulsion to quickly and easily shift into a new particle reality. Your higher self is offering you a brand-new life, and if you choose wisely, you will spend the next half of your life exhilarated by new opportunities.

Numerology Personal Years

One last yearly cycle worth noting is the numerology personal year. Each year is marked by a cycle from 1-9. It is calculated by using your birth month + birthday + current year. These cycles begin on January 1st and end on December 31st. To calculate the personal year, we go through a process of reduction and addition. The number 11 and 22 are NOT reduced because they are master numbers. So, my birthday is November 12th, and the current year is 2017: November being an 11, which is not reduced, then 12 reduces to a 3 and 2017 reduces to a 10/1. So, 11+3 = 14 + 1 = 15/6. 6 is the number of Venus, and it resonates with relationships of all kinds. The focus is on attracting, improving, and harmonizing. Hence, this was the perfect year to finish my relationship book! Another example is May 12th in the year 2017 Added up it looks like: 5 + 3 = 8 +1 = 9.

9 is the end of a numerology cycle. I particularly like seeing clients who are in a 9 or 1 cycle because I can give them important guidance that may go unnoticed. A 9 year lets me know they are tying up loose ends. I liken it to tilling up a garden, and ridding yourself of weeds. Anything that doesn't support upcoming growth is discarded. People often finish relationships in a 9 year. Following a 9 year is the 1 year, which reminds me of planting seeds

in a garden. It is a time of renewed growth and lots of brand new beginnings. When I see a client in a 1 year, I strongly encourage them to start as many new things as possible. This isn't a year for completion; it's a year for preparing the next 9-year cycle of life.

New doorways are always opening in our lives, but they take courage to walk through to the other side. Many people level off when they are met with these intense pushes to grow. They may stuff down the inspiration and quietly assume their "fate." They may stay in unhealthy marriages and miserable jobs for decades. They refuse to budge because they do not want to leave their comfort zones, even though comfort has become a noose tied around their necks. Eventually, chronic illness swoops in, forcing them to make necessary changes.

There are a few renegades who courageously and dramatically walk through the doors and alter their lives. They throw off their shackles! They shift personalities and move into new particle realities. As they shift, and those around them do not, they appear unknown, crazy, irresponsible, & erratic. The term "mid-life crisis" enters here. If the people in their lives do not match the new particle reality, these people move out of the renegade's life. Mismatched spouses become estranged and then divorced. Activity with abrasive family members diminishes or fades out.

Exercise XV. Beyond Fairytales

Beginning with your earliest childhood memory, all the way up to your current life situation, list your unlived dreams. As you review this list, KNOW that most, if not all, of these dreams, can still manifest. Also, take responsibility for the fact that no one besides you kept your dreams from fully materializing.

Reflection:

How did this list make you feel? Sad? Angry? Relieved? Excited? Did the act of taking responsibility for these unlived dreams stir you to pursue them?

Exercise XVI. Evolving Roles

During chaotic, tumultuous life changes, you can work with the field, rather than rebel against it. Just as in Exercise VIII, "The Field of Dreams," you may create positive scenarios of your existing relationships. We'll pretend your 24-year-old daughter, Sam is leaving home. Her attitude is rebellious and confrontational. You wonder where your sweet little girl went. In this example, her personality seems to have changed, while yours did not. She probably thinks the same of you! Remember you always create your perception of your reality. Underneath the drama of the moment, you may find your own feelings of unease, fear, & loss which inspires this behavior from her.

When you sense a change in a relationship, first acknowledge change is a necessity for continued growth & happiness. Next, intend to accept the new identities and dynamics being birthed. In the case of an emerging adult child, it is your job to gradually shift from the role of protective, authority parent into the role of good, supportive friend. Anything short of shifting identities may cause undue strain on the remaining relationship.

For parents who initially created an imbalanced, enmeshed relationship with their child, this shift in roles can be excessively painful, especially when the child goes on to raise their own family. The parent may be left feeling betrayed and abandoned. However, if the parent is unwilling to evolve the relationship with their child, the adult child will meet with tremendous difficulty in establishing healthy, adult roles as parents and as spouses. The remaining parent/child relationship will also be unduly strained.

I agree it will be difficult to suddenly forget you knew this woman when she was wearing diapers. However, by clinging to that past timeline, you will unconsciously carry over old ingrained patterns. You will automatically act like the all-knowing authority, and she may perceive that as your lack of trust in her own judgement. These perspectives are not encouraged by fully grown adults and will meet with great resistance. The resistance is your mirror that change is needed.

Once you can easily accept a shift in roles, you are ready to create joyful scenes of you and your daughter enjoying each other's new relationship. To make this exercise potently effective, do it in 2 parts: The first part involves writing a perfect scene from a day in your harmonious relationship. The second part involves drawing a picture of this scene.

Part I: Write a scene like a movie trailer: including weather, location, dialogue, characters (you & your daughter as great, loving friends), and action. Go into the scene, feel it fully and talk from a first-person vantage point.

Example: It's 11 am, and Sam & I are going to a spa for facials and full body massages. As we are sitting in the salon chairs, I look over at her and feel gratitude for the woman she has become. I particularly enjoy her company. She has her own thoughts & preferences, and I really like it that she's not a clone of me. I treat her with the respect of a cherished friend and never overstep my boundaries with unsolicited advice or criticism. We get along so well! She treats me with loving respect and genuine appreciation for the woman I am. I really like this new kind of relationship with her, because for once, I finally feel like she sees me as a human being!

Part II: After the written version is completed, you may now draw the scene. The picture itself is not as important as the feelings the drawing evokes in you. Be creative & colorful! While these exercises can be done anytime, the manifestation is more potent when they are done just before bedtime.

Reflection:

Did swapping roles from authority parent to cherished friend feel threatening to you? Why do you think that is? Paradoxically, did this scene feel more real than reality? (In this moment of focused attention, it is.) Can you see how this shift in you automatically shifts the relationship? Can you see how a new role will enrich your relationship?

Personal Growth While Maintaining Important Relationships

Here's where it gets tricky because people get caught in certain relationship dynamics and continue them throughout the life of the relationship. Years later, they come to expect certain patterns and disallow change in that dynamic. As energy is constantly changing, and we are made of energy, we all have the opportunity for change and growth. Will we take it? That's a free will choice. The key is to balance personal growth with the evolvement of our relationship.

When people choose to relocate, they can become anyone they choose to be. Why? Because the environment has no history with them. When we stay in familiar surroundings for years, with the same people around us, we subconsciously receive certain expectations from those around us. It goes both ways, too. We maintain certain expectations toward people in our lives.

I see so many people in their empty nest stage, who decide to begin a spiritual quest. They start attending workshops, reading books, and expanding their consciousness. However, their spouse is seldom involved in these ventures. What happens? The expanding individual thinks the spouse is "stuck" and refusing to change. Guess how the "stuck" spouse feels? They feel threatened and abandoned. This is normal when any relationship changes.

Obviously, no two people are going to share the same exact interests. One partner may love gardening, while the other partner may love car racing. I see these differences cause the most difficulty when one partner is seeking spiritual evolvement, while the other is not. Yes, there will be times when you just cannot find a meeting ground with a person. However, in most cases, two people, who truly want to be together, can find more harmony than disharmony.

If you are in a long-term relationship, and you are awakening spiritually, realize the knowledge you are learning is not what is changing the relationship. The vibrational shifting is what causes the feeling of brakes scraping metal, but it doesn't have to remain that way. In your growth, your vibration is shifting to a higher frequency. This is good for both partners! The highest vibration is love. As you are shifting to a purer frequency of love, you can shower that vibration on your mate, who can then shift to a higher frequency. Reading spiritual books and attending workshops is not necessary to shift to a higher frequency.

Do you want to know what most folks do when they choose a new spiritual path? They start looking for all the flaws in their mate. "Why is she so stuck?" "Why is he so pessimistic?" "He only brings me down!" Instead of focusing on their shifts, they try to start fixing their partner. This causes even more resistance in the partner, who is already threatened by the changes in their mate. As we've discovered in the preceding exercises, you do the work quietly on yourself, and your partner either comes along or not.

Blaming and criticizing your mate isn't going to get you anywhere that you want to be. For the harmony and longevity of the relationship, it doesn't really matter if your mate ever learns to meditate, talk about new age concepts or attend a workshop. Sure, you may want them to do these things, but this isn't the make or break point in the relationship. The only thing that matters here is a matching frequency. You may meditate on a mountain rock to find your connection to Source. Your mate may carve wood to find his connection. I suspect a lot of evolving people fear their mate will somehow suck them back down in consciousness. No worries, because: *once you know, you know.* Yes, you can entertain lower frequencies, but the consciousness that has shifted will not return to the pre-evolved status in a single lifetime.

Recently, a man came to me for shaman work. He'd been married 15 years to one of his soul mates, but the relationship was a long, volatile roller coaster. His wife had lots of addiction troubles. While he encouraged his wife to join in the shamanic work (smart man), she refused. So, I worked with him, and he quickly realigned with his truth. However, once his vibration shifted, he was no longer able to tolerate the abusive dynamic. He and his wife were no longer a vibrational match. At this point, his wife had a choice to make: she could get help, or their marriage would be over. He worked his exercises, but there wasn't a matching healthy version of his wife. Sadly, they separated.

The old drama no longer sufficed, but it wasn't my shifted client who left. It was the spouse who needed the dysfunction. She could not tolerate the higher frequency and chose to leave. Relationship endings do happen even with shifting work. What this tells me is that one partner has graduated from the lessons of the relationship, while the other partner still has healing work to do, perhaps with another partner.

Exercise XVII. How do I trap my partner?

Guess what? This exercise gives you the first opportunity to really complain about your partner!!!! Don't pop the champagne bottle too fast. For everything you see as "wrong," you will own as your creation.

In this exercise, you will examine how your own perceptions pull certain behaviors from your mate. Make a list of 3 columns. Label column #1 "I dislike," label column #2: "How much I complain (about dislike)" and column #3 "Good things he/she already changed." For example, I write under #1: My husband leaves dirty dishes in the sink. Then under column #2, I write, "every other day." Lastly, I write his change under #3, "returns the scissors to the kitchen drawer."

As you reflected on how often you complain about your mate's disliked behavior, were you aware that the complaining is magnetizing more unwanted actions towards you? Did you recognize that your mate has been able to change things in the past and can change again?

Exercise XVIII. What I adore about you

Now, we're going to clean up the energy of the last exercise.

I was once told that you could make a complimentary list about a person with 25 points, each being positive, except one, and the complimented person will focus on the ONE negative point. That's how much weight criticism carries. Criticism magnetically attracts more to criticize. Of course, you will dislike things about your mate.

Rather than criticizing, learn to reframe the negative into the positive that you do like.

So, in this exercise, you will learn to start making daily appreciation lists of your mate. Begin by looking at your "dislike" column from the above exercise. Flip the negative into a positive statement in the present tense. Example: I dislike my husband leaving dirty dishes in the sink. New statement: I love having a clean kitchen with dishes in the dishwasher. (Notice, we are not saying how the dirty dishes get out of the sink, we are only acknowledging them being gone). After you've rewritten all your disliked points, now you can start fresh with a list of all the wonderful qualities in your mate. Do this exercise alone until you can get a good hold on the new vibration of appreciation. Then you can share your mate's positive qualities with them. Eventually, you may even do this exercise as a couple. Don't make it a chore; keep it light and loving. Heaps of compliments magically create change in our mates.

Reflection:

Did you notice your love growing as you listed your mate's positive qualities? By focusing on what you desire, it grows the desirable. Pay attention. In the glow of your admiration, your mate will probably start giving you more things to appreciate!

Chapter Seven
Endings: Death & Separations

But our love it was stronger by far... ☆
☆ *And neither the angels in Heaven above*
Nor the demons down under the sea ☆
Can ever dissever my soul from the soul
☆ *Of the beautiful Annabel Lee* ☆ ☆
"Annabel Lee," Edgar Allen Poe

Let the Butterfly Transform Itself

Change always involves loss. Learning to accept loss is one of man's greatest challenges. When we are truly attached to another being, such as a spouse, family member, child, friend, pet or soul mate, we may dread their eventual death. I've had the blessing of knowing lifetime happily married couples, who's vows lasted 40+ years. I've witnessed the death of their partners, and it was truly heart breaking.

However, death is not the end of the personality or the relationship. The transition into death is but a gossamer thread between realities. We think of these realities as far-away, unreachable places, but they are as close as pages in a book. Through the exercises under Soul Mating, we have learned to pierce the veil of physical separation by actively directing energy. Thus, we may continue our relationships after death without pause. The only thing lost in the death transition is the physical form. The love, personal energy signature, communications, relatedness, memories, and consciousness are all still very much alive. In fact, the relationship connection is at its very best in death because all resistant, negative thought patterns have been wiped clean. You never truly know a person until they die because resistant vibrational patterns cloud the soul's light during earthly form. There is one caveat to this purity though, there are those souls who become entrapped in Earth's vibrational pull, and unfortunately, they have not yet shed their humanly flaws. Through our previous advanced psychic training exercises, we can discern which ones have been purified, and which ones have not.

As human beings in specifically unique and distinct body forms, we tend to define our souls, our God, our angels, and our demons into very distinct physical forms. The finiteness of reality only exists here. Remember: our 3D-reality is the only place where physical manifestation takes on a lingering physical form. As your loved one crosses beyond 3D-reality, they do not lose themselves. Do not fear that your loved one has become "swallowed up" into infinity. In spirit, as in earthly life, they still maintain their energy signature. The solid earthly form is all that's missing.

Exercise XIX. Awake & Listening

This exercise will only be applicable after you've had adequate time to grieve the loss of your loved one. The frequency of grief is very low vibrationally; this does not imply "wrongness;" it's just a different frequency range. In the vibration of grief, you do not yet have access to your transitioned loved one. Thus, you will not be able to match the transitioned souls who are now very high, light energy beings until your energy shifts to a higher vibration. When you can get yourself to a peaceful, hopeful, or joyful place and still think of your loved one, you're ready to do this exercise.

In these exercises, first call on God, "God, Creator of All Things, it is requested that I have interactions with the highest version of (your loved one's name). I ask that all interactions be graced by your love and light. Thank you."

Part I: Imagine yourself standing before your loved one, and see them radiantly happy and talking to you. Imagine their favorite body language, sound, laugh, or phrase. Look in their eyes and say, "I choose to allow our relationship to expand and evolve. Please send me a clear sign to let me know you are listening." After this energy interaction, pay attention: many signs come through smells and animal messengers. Signs can come from anywhere. Pay attention to dreams because transitioned souls often make visits during dreamtime.

Part II: On repeating this exercise, ask your loved one for a hug. You will feel the most joyful feeling coming from the inside out.

Part III: Create a common scene for you and your loved one to routinely visit, such as a porch swing or a kitchen table. See yourself sitting and enjoying a conversation. What is said? How does it feel?

Reflection:

Did you feel love and support flowing from your loved one? Did you receive important guidance? How did they feel to you?

Death or Separation from a Soul Mate

> *And I wondered, as I cleared away our tea cups*
> *Why are your eyes so familiar? They are ocean green*
> *And his were…dark brown*
> *But why is something behind your eyes –so familiar?*
> *Your features are not familiar at all—at least, not yet*
> *They are still the features of a stranger I've known*
> *Only a short time*
> *But the eyes….are so familiar*

Gooberz, Linda Goodman

After finding another person with whom you feel such a strong connection, it can be excruciatingly painful to separate from that person in any loss, especially death. The loss is devastating and can take a long time to heal. Famous literature is marked by soul mate separations, such as the Edgar Allen Poe poem, "Annabel Lee." Although I haven't experienced the death of a soul mate, I have experienced many instances of separation. I struggled to understand how such intensely anticipated love could be lost through separation or death. It seemed like such a waste. For several years, I lived with a wish to understand, until the answers finally came to me.

Linda Goodman suspected that death of a soul mate was conquerable. She hinted at her theory in her novel, <u>Gooberz</u>. She noticed as she was looking in the eyes of a lover that she recognized a familiarity. She concluded it was a walk-in of her transitioned soul mate. Walk-ins are disembodied souls who contract to inhabit a vacated body. I scoured her novel as well as many other soul mate books, looking for every single clue I could find about separations from soul mates. However, the walk-in theory never quite gelled for me. While I do believe walk-ins exist, I do not believe it is a common occurrence. I did however, believe Linda was right that soul mate death is conquerable.

Unexpectedly the answer came to me. I was watching an Abraham-Hicks video about a man losing his dog. As they began to speak of soul families, fireworks sparkled in my mind! The love isn't lost! That was the very first moment I made the decision to write this book. As I continued to learn about quantum physics, my mind framed it all into a very plausible theory.

In instances of incomplete love, separations, or death, we need not fear loss. We may find comfort in attracting a new person of the same soul family group essence. Within the soul family groups, there are smaller groupings of souls who share similar soul essences. When we meet one of these people, they are so strikingly similar that we feel we've known them before. Thus, within our pool of soul mates, we can a) attract another soul mate relationship from our soul family or b) attract another soul mate who matches the essence of our lost soul mate lover. Thus, nothing is ever truly lost.

Think in terms of particles. Earlier, we worked through exercises to tap into different versions of self as well as loved ones. These exercises seem impossible to do when we know a person has "died" or permanently left. As an example, let's say you had a dearly loved daughter who suddenly, unexpectedly died. After a year or more of processing your grief, you begin shifting your way to a better, higher frequency. One day, you decide to take art classes. Your teacher comes in, and there's an unmistakable familiarity about her. You watch this beautiful, sensitive, caring young woman. She talks to you, and you feel chills rush up your spine. You think, "This is exactly who my daughter would've grown up to be. She feels exactly like her." You have just met one of your daughter's multiple soul essence personalities.

As you open to manifesting a newer version of your lost loved one, this new person may or may not look the same as the lost. Their timeline will be different. Their personality will be different. The relationship will be very different. However, you will know them by their essence alone, and you will feel an irresistible pull toward them. They too, will feel the same strong pull of recognition. However, they may not choose to move forward based on soul recognition alone. Put your focus on manifesting what is in your highest soul's intention and see what develops. One of the reasons the other person left your reality may be because the lessons were completed. Don't try to force anything. Just be curious.

Peering through gray hair, the old Chinese palm reader looked up from my hand and whispered, "Let love transform like a butterfly."

Exercise XX. The Transformed Butterfly

As in the previous exercise, this exercise will only be possible once you've processed your grief and are able to focus on your soul mate in a positive, joyful attitude.

Go into meditation and ask God to show you another matching version of your soul mate. Ask if there is a version of reality where you two are together. Get very still and quiet, and allow the vision to come. Don't try to manage what you receive. Watch for a person to appear. Do you see yourself together?

Next, notice how this person feels. Do they feel like the "lost" soul mate? If they do not feel like the person you knew, they may be a new soul mate coming in. Ask your guides if this is another soul mate.

If you see yourself together with this person, you have two choices: you may follow this vision to see how you'd interact with this new soul mate, OR you can dismiss the visual, begin again, asking for a soul essence match of your lost soul mate. Please note that you may have completed your intentions with this essence, in which case, it will be most beneficial to accept the gift of a new soul mate energy.

Do not let appearances throw you. The body is but a shell that encases the soul. The most important detail is the feeling of familiarity. View the scene, as though you were watching a movie. Absorb as many details as possible. Once you've completed this exercise with confirmation of togetherness, I advise you to return to Exercise IX, "You, the Movie Director" and build scenes based on this newly received information. You will be setting up the energetic matrix to call in your new mate. Don't worry about where, how or when you will meet, just know this person is a potential particle reality. Only concern yourself with shifting into that new particle reality where this person lives. Here's where your real work will come in. The help of a spiritual advisor is recommended to guide you through releasing the former relationship in favor of moving into your new relationship.

Reflection:

How did it feel to recognize a similar vibration placed in a different human body? You are learning that energy is not trapped by its form. Energy never dies; it only transforms.

Choosing to Leave Your Relationship

> *Anyone who moves out of your experience for any reason was not a match to the wonderful future that is waiting for you in vibrational escrow.*
>
> *The Astonishing Power of Emotions, Esther & Jerry Hicks*

There will be times when you desire to leave a relationship behind. If you've put all the energy into the relationship that you choose to give, then please do not feel like a failure for walking away. Remember, there are no right or wrong choices. You hear people say of divorce, "His failed marriage." Just because a relationship ends, does not make it a failure. A failure by who's standards? I say, if you grew from the experience, which you did, the relationship was a complete success—even if it lasted 2 hours or 25 years.

Relationships with spouses, lovers, friends, family members, or colleagues, may be too loaded with negativity to desire or even expect a shift. While you may know exactly why you want to leave, at other times, you might not understand the need to walk away. That's ok! It may be months or years before you fully understand why you needed to leave.

While editing this chapter, a beautiful Pisces Southern Belle called about her marriage. The question was simple, "Is my husband cheating?" Although I did not find the man to be cheating, yet, I did see him in major need of a life overhaul. As a Sagittarius, his motivation rests in chasing the next new dream. Dreams keep him young and vital. What does a new sex partner evoke? Excitement, passion, hope. The same as a new dream. I could see the potential for a break in their marriage, but I also saw the ability to transform the old relationship style completely. This wise Pisces intuited things were on the rocks and reached out for a fresh perspective. I gave her the exercises in this book. I encouraged her to script a revitalized happy marriage, with her husband living a new dream. We shall see what transpires!

While all the passages and exercises in this book are meant to give you an alternative approach to relationships, they are not meant to sway you from your good common sense and survival needs. In abusive relationships, you may not have time to spend shifting yourself or the relationship. In all cases, if your emotional, physical or mental health are in jeopardy, please leave the situation as quickly as possible.

Once you've made the decision to terminate a relationship, focus your intention immediately on cleaning up the negative residue left from the relationship. DO work the exercises. Remember, you can always leave a relationship, but you will carry the dominant vibration it invoked in you. Harping on wrongs only hurts your reality because lower vibration emotions will extend into other areas of your life. Have you ever been on a date with a newly separated person? Most of the date is spent reviewing all the traumas the ex-spouse inflicted on them. Does this type of conversation entice you to continue dating this person? Well, only if misery loves company!

There are people who have no problem making breaks, but they hate to be alone; so, they will prolong leaving until they've secured another relationship. This is not a good practice because you merely repeat the unresolved patterns with the new mate. By taking "down time" between relationships, you get a chance to make necessary shifts. It is much easier to shift into a new you when you are single.

Transitioning Out of a Relationship

> And ruined love, when it is built anew,
> Grows fairer than at first, more strong, far greater.
> So I return rebuked to my content,
> And gain by ills thrice more than I have spent.
>
> "Shake-Spears Sonnets Never Before Imprinted: Sonnet #119,"
> Shakespeare

If your current relationship has reached a level of catastrophic destruction, and you still don't want to give up, you may need to temporarily separate, to accomplish your shifting goals. This happens a lot more than suspected in marriages. The couple takes a break to separate and sometimes divorce. Then a funny thing happens! They find their way back to each other. How is this possible? In their separation, they drop a lot of resistance and begin shifting to a different version of themselves. They may reinvent their image. They may find a new passion. They may change their work. In any case, their shifted self attracts their spouse back to them. On both ends, the heavy negativity clouding the marriage is released, and both partners find a new level of appreciation for each other. This outcome can easily happen if you're doing the shifting work during the separation.

When you are in a relationship, you are often distracted by what is happening in the relationship; if it is disagreeable, you're easily hypnotized by this pattern. As previously discussed, it is completely possible to shift while in a relationship, but you will need your mind to be singly focused in the direction of your new reality. After I hung up with my Pisces client, I text her: "Do your best to take attention off what he's doing. Put ALL your attention on creating the marriage you want."

Exercise XXI. Preparing for the Break

Obviously, most people do not want to hear the words "I think we should take some time," or "I want a divorce," or "I think we should just be friends." Terminating relationships often feels like abandonment and rejection by the person being left behind. To soften negative reactions, you can telepathically talk to the other person before the actual physical interaction.

Imagine standing in front of the other person. Place one hand over your heart area while looking in the other person's eyes. Speak your words of choosing to move on. Thank the person for the lessons they've taught you and for helping you to understand yourself more. Even if this relationship was painful for you to endure, I highly recommend speaking the positive of it to yourself and the other person. By seeing the positive benefits, you clean up negative debris and make way for something better to come in.

You may be feeling all sorts of emotions, like anger, betrayal, sadness, or boredom when you decide to move away from a person. You've undoubtedly already rehearsed conversations in your mind. Those conversations may have been laced with a lot of hurt and blame. Make no doubt, your words were telepathically received by the other person. While the average person will not know what you said telepathically, they will feel a vague sense of unease toward you. Don't be surprised if you are avoided altogether or receive unexpected gifts and declarations of love. This is *very* common.

With this exercise, you are focusing on what it is you want to achieve in the break. This exercise is not about vengeance, blame, or denial. It is simply preparing the way for a clean break, so that you may go on to create what your heart truly desires. You may repeat this exercise until you feel peaceful about the upcoming conversation. As you've pre-paved the actual conversation, the other person will not feel ambushed or shocked. They may even beat you to the punch by breaking it off first.

As you were speaking to your mate, how did they react? Did you feel resistance or peace? When you can feel peaceful, you are ready to physically take the next step.

Dating Again

As you begin dating again, notice the various people who attract your attention. Do they each follow a common thread? If you notice a pattern, what is it? Is it a positive pattern or a negative one? If negative, what does this pattern reveal about your own issues? During my single years, I noticed a continual pattern of soul mate attractions. I also realized many of these soul mates were closet gay/bisexual men who were raised by dominant, enmeshing mothers. Additionally, they each had strong Scorpio/Pluto influences in their astrology charts. Our interactions were mostly platonic, with very few sexual liaisons. I kept asking myself, "Why am I attracting these kinds of men? What's going on here?"

In my life, I had several relationships with dominant, enmeshing mother figures. This lifetime wound created a vibrational field around me that called in others with similar issues. Children raised in enmeshed parent/child relationships, play the role of spouse to their enmeshing parent. Invariably, these relationships carry a strong sexual component, whether overt sexual abuse ever happens or not. Fear of intimacy runs deep. As mentioned, each of my soul mate exchanges involved heavy Scorpio influences. Scorpio energy grows up in an extremely intense, sexually charged environment, where the adults play manipulative games to get their needs met. Thus, the issues arising in my exchanges centered around power struggles involving sex energy.

Your pattern could be involved with married women, non-committal men, addicts, or abuse victims. The pattern could be anything, but the most important thing for you to consider is this: what does this pattern reflect in my vibration? If this isn't a positive pattern, what in me needs to shift? I guarantee you, if you do not shift beyond this personality trait, you will continue to go through this pattern in relationships.

Speaking of repeating patterns, an evolved, male client of mine continued to call me with each new soul mate, exclaiming, "This one is different! She's the one!" As his life coach and shaman, I was noticing a pattern. Each female carried tremendous baggage from previous abuse; each female came on hot and heavy and then ran away. All his women refused to heal. So, I asked him, "Tell me about your childhood and your relationship with your parents." He began, "My mom was always in abusive relationships. My parents were separated. When I was 14, my dad took me to live with him because he was tired of all the drama my mom kept me in." I asked, "How did you feel when you went to live with him?" Introspectively, he replied, "I felt really guilty that I couldn't save her." I offered, "Do you think that maybe you are attracting these unhealthy women as a way of saving your mom?" He reflected and replied, "You know, I never thought about it that way. Explains a lot." Unconsciously, he was trying to heal an unresolved childhood wound.

Interestingly, people who aren't living their soul-purpose of healer and spiritual guide, will unconsciously apply their talents in places they don't belong. They turn their personal relationships into client/healer relationships; their lovers become clients! Romantic relationships especially, are not the place to act as a healer. I know, it is a romanticized, Hollywood idea, to rescue and heal a lover. It is not. It swiftly degrades the relationship into a very dysfunctional, codependent pattern. We are not capable of remaining objective when our heart is concerned. If you notice this pattern in yourself, release the lover to a professional healer or therapist, and save your together time for true relating. What's true relating? It's two equal people choosing togetherness because they enjoy each other. It's not about spending time trying to heal old baggage.

During my single years, I watched certain astrology signs cycle in and out, as stated above with my trend in Scorpio dominant love interests. I've noticed with clients that they often attract certain astrology signs. Some clients have told me, "I always end up with

Cancers," or "I've married 3 Pisces." Although there's much more to astrology than just Sun signs, I wanted to make a list for you to investigate what your astrology attractions mean:

When attracting:

Aries: You need a courageous new beginning; you have projects to start. The Aries will light a fire under you!

Taurus: Sensual, grounded physical care is essential; a time for sound money management. Taurus brings you out of the clouds and down to practical earth.

Gemini: Lighten up, and be more social! Explore new things, communicate more. Gemini inspires youthful inquisitiveness.

Cancer: Home is where your heart is now. Focus on domestication. Cancer wants to nest. Looking for a mother figure?

Leo: Don't be afraid to shine! Appreciate your talents. Toot your own horn! Leo enjoys showing you off because they are proud of you. Be proud of you too!

Virgo: Pay attention to the details. Diet and exercise are important. Virgo shows you where there are problems and helps you find solutions.

Libra: Learn how to be harmonious, fair and balanced without giving yourself away. Commit to a decision. Libra teaches you manners and how to charm people.

Scorpio: Your life is needing a major transformation. What are power struggles really trying to tell you? You may attract this mate when you are feeling reckless, so you seek someone who will bring order to your life. Also, Scorpio is a powerful, fearless guide during crisis periods and teaches you how to be the phoenix rising from the ashes.

Sagittarius: Take a trip abroad, study a new philosophy or culture. Go back to college. Embrace freedom. Time to drop all codependency patterns, Sag won't stand for it!

Capricorn: Good business management and strong leadership are necessary. If you're an entrepreneur, take some sound advice from powerful Capricorn. Looking for a father figure?

Aquarius: Friendship is very important for lasting relationship; don't rush into commitment before this foundation is built. Aquarius also checks possessiveness. Lessons will be learned in authenticity.

Pisces: An introduction into the nebulous, fluid realm of spirit. Start a new spiritual program involving prayer and meditation. Sublime creativity is enhanced. Be careful with mood altering substances.

In Closing

The magical tools you've learned on these pages can be applied to every area of your life. You can do similar energy molding on your career, your appearance, your health, your spirituality, your creativity and any other subject that matters to you. Chances are very strong that many of these areas did shift during your relationship shifting work. Your ability to manifest your dreams has just increased exponentially because you now understand how manifestations occur.

I want to extend my most heartfelt and humble gratitude to my husband, Matt, and to all the clients who helped fill these pages. I'd also like to extend my appreciation to Neville Goddard, who was quoted in these pages. He made a surprise dream visit during the editing of this book. He wrote a sweet comment and signed the inner cover. What a confirmation and blessing from one of my teachers!

At any moment, a quantum shift can happen—expect it!

☆

☆

☆   ☆

☆

☆

Afterword

Every day, I talk to many of you who are struggling with relationship issues. Throughout these pages, we have discovered magical tools that can help you create powerful changes in your relationships. The desire and effort to make those changes, rest on you. You may not wish to continue some relationships, while you may want to give your very best efforts to others.

With all the struggles I've witnessed in relationships, my deepest wish for you is to find joy and peace in all your relationships. Many of you are real troopers who will hang on until the bitter end, no matter what you endure. You sacrifice your life and your happiness hoping for a change. You put up with broken promises, disrespect, lack of commitment, and verbal abuse. While the tools in this book do work, you owe it to yourself to choose the healthiest path for you. I've had clients wait 5, 10, 20 years for a person to shift. Please don't waste your life on someone who is not a match to your dream. Do the exercises, make the shifts, but also commit to a timeline when you will walk away from chronically unhealthy situations. Sometimes, the changes come by leaving a relationship. I'm very aware that some people will cling to unhealthy conditions the minute the shift reveals an ending. At the threat of loss, some will drop the changes and revert to old patterns, just to hang on to a fading relationship. Trust yourself. Trust the universe. You deserve to be honored and loved.

Ultimately, this book is about choosing You. As you continue to heal, grow, and shift, the right people will be in your life. Promise.

This above all: to thine own self be true. Shakespeare

Sending you Many Mystical Blessings,

Brenda Renee', Mystical Empress

Bibliography

Arntz, William; Chasse, Betsy; Vicente, Mark, What the Bleep Do We Know!? Down the Rabbit Hole. United States: Samuel Goldwyn Films, 2004

Boel, Cornelis, King James Bible. 1611

Carroll, Lewis, Alice's Adventures in Wonderland. United Kingdom: MacMillan, 1865

Choquette, Sonia, Diary of a Psychic. Carlsbad, California: Hay House, Inc., 2003

Gibran, Kahlil, The Prophet. United States: Alfred A. Knopf, 1923

Goddard, Neville, Awakened Imagination. Camarillo, California: De Vorss Publications, 1954

Goddard, Neville, The Power of Awareness. Camarillo, California: De Vorss Publications, 1952

Goodman, Linda, Gooberz. Norfolk, Virginia: Hampton Roads Publishing Company, Inc., 1989

Goodman, Linda, Linda Goodman's Star Signs. New York: St Martin's Press, 1987

Goodman, Linda, Venus Trines at Midnight. Taplinger Publishing Company, 1970

Grimm, Brothers, Grimm's Fairytales. Germany: Brothers Grimm, 1854

Hicks, Esther & Jerry, Ask and It Is Given. Carlsbad, California: Hay House, Inc., 2004

Hicks, Esther & Jerry, The Astonishing Power of Emotions. Carlsbad, California: Hay House, Inc., 2007

Hollis, James, The Eden Project: In Search of the Magical Order. Ontario, Canada: Inner City Books, 1998

Jung, Carl, The Collected Works of C.G. Jung. New York, New York: Bollingen Foundation, Inc, 1957

Poe, Edgar Allen, Annabel Lee. Richmond, Virginia: Southern Literary Messenger, 1849

Poe, Edgar Allen, The Raven and Other Poems. New York: Wiley Putnam, 1845

Roberts, Jane, Seth Speaks. New York: Bantam Books, 1972

Roberts, Jane, The Nature of Personal Reality. Englewood Cliffs, New Jersey: Prentice-Hall, Inc., 1974

Shakespeare, William, A Midsummer Night's Dream. London: Thomas Fisher, 1600

Shakespeare, William, First Folio: As You Like It, London: 1623

Shakespeare, William, Shake-Spears Sonnets Never Before Imprinted. London: Thomas Thorpe, 1609

Shakespeare, William, The Tragedy of Hamlet, Prince of Denmark. London: Nicholas Ling, 1603

Siberry, Jane, It Can't Rain All the Time, The Crow Original Motion Picture Soundtrack, 1994

Sparks, Nicholas, The Notebook. United States: Time Warner Book Group, 1996

De Troyes, Chrétien, Lancelot, the Knight of the Cart, 1177

Tzu Lao, Tao te Ching: 4000BCE

De Villeneuve, Barbot Suzanne Gabrielle, La Belle et La Bete. France: Jeanne-Marie le Prince de Beaumont, 1740

Yogananda, Parahamansa, Autobiography of a Yogi. United States: The Philosophical Library, 1946

About the Author

Mystical Empress Brenda Renee' holds a Bachelor's of Liberal Arts in Legal Studies, a Masters in Metaphysics, and professional certification in Feng Shui. She is an astrologer, shaman, Feng Shui practitioner, horticulturist, artist, actress, and intuitive. She has written for various new age magazines, such as *Indigo Sun*, *Transformations*, and her monthly *"Feng Shui Q&A"* for *Delta Style Magazine*. She's spent 19 years in private consulting & teaching. She partners with God, angelic helpers, totem animals, the plant & mineral kingdom, star beings, and the fairy realm in her consulting, writing and workshops.

The Mystical Empress guides her clients with a tapestry of creative, holistic, spiritual talents that are woven into her: shamanism, quantum life coaching, intuitive readings, astrological charts and Feng Shui consultations. She shows you how easy it is to blend quantum energy techniques into your personal needs and dreams! She is a powerful spiritual guide for your soul's path. To learn more about Mystical Empress Brenda Renee's services & workshops, please go to www.mysticalempress.com or write Brenda Renee' at Brenda@mysticalempress.com